a 15-session course on the
fundamentals of reincarnation
based upon Sha'ar HaGilgulim
of the Arizal

fundamentals of reincarnation

thirtysix.org

Fundamentals of Reincarnation

A course about the fundamentals of reincarnation
based upon Sha'ar HaGilgulim from the Arizal

ISBN 9781520980881

Published by:
Thirtysix.org
355 St. Clair Avenue W.
Toronto, Ontario
Canada   M5P 1N5

We would like to dedicate this important work from Rabbi Pinchas Winston to our children, Aliza, Yoel, Refael Meir & Arieh. It is our hope that they will merit to see and live in a world of peace, and experience na-chat from growing in Torah and chesed. May we be merit to see the coming of Mo-shiach very soon.

Lea & Chaim A. Bitton M.D
Geneva, Switzerland

contents

KABBALAH TRACES ITS origin back in time to Moshe Rabbeinu, and even earlier. According to many, Sefer Yetzirah, one of the greatest Kabbalistic works of all time, was authored by Avraham Avinu. Even Migdal Bavel,[1] according to tradition, was built according to Kabbalistic specifications.[2]

Rabbi Shimon bar Yochai, of the Second Temple period, is considered to be the source of the Zohar, the main body of Kabbalah literature, even though it wasn't officially published until the 1300s. The Rashbi[3] had taught a select group of

---

[1] The Tower of Bavel.
[2] Hakdamos u'Sha'arim, Sha'ar 7, Ch. 6:5.
[3] An acronym for Rabbi Shimon bar Yochai.

students the tradition he had received from his teachers, which included the great Rebi Akiva.

It wasn't until the 16th century and Rabbi Yitzchak Luria, otherwise known as the Arizal, that Kabbalah became a lot more accessible. It was the notes of his premier student, Rabbi Chaim Vital, that became the basis of the "Kisvei Arizal," the "Writings of the Arizal." Sha'ar HaGilgulim, or the "Gate of Reincarnations," is the last of these eight volumes, and the basis of this course.

The goal of this work has been to make these ideas even more accessible. These 15 lessons can only be, however, the starting point for anyone who truly wants to better understand the concept of reincarnation and personal rectification.

one
what is pardes?

A PARDES IN everyday life is an orchard, as in a piece of land planted with fruit trees. In the realm of Torah, however, specifically on the level of Kabbalah,[1] the word refers to an "orchard" of a different nature:

> There are four levels [of Torah] interpretation. Their "sign" is [the Hebrew word] "Pardes," and [they are called]: Pshat, Remez, Drush, and Sod. (Sha'ar HaGilgulim, Introduction 11)

By "sign" he means a mnemonic, a memory device comprised of four letters: Peh, Raish, Dalet,

---

[1] Torah mysticism.

and Samech, that when combined, "happen" to form the word "pardes." Each letter however is also the first letter[2] of a different word, each of which is the name of a different level of Torah learning.

S	Sod	Secret
D	Drush	Exegesis
R	Remez	Hint
P	Pshat	Simple

Pardes & The Four Levels
of Torah Learning

The best way to understand what each level means is through an example. The first verse of the Torah says:

> In the beginning, God made the heaven and the earth. (Bereishis 1:1)

The Pshat of anything is its simplest and most obvious explanation. In the case of this verse it is that, at the beginning of everything, God first made the heaven and the earth. As Rashi[3] points out, however, there is something about the Hebrew text that "hints" to another level of explanation:

> The Torah did not come to teach the sequence of creating, to say what came first. If it had come to teach this it should have written: "At

---

[2] This is called "roshei teivos" in Hebrew, literally, "heads of words."
[3] Shlomo Yitzchaki (1040–1105) was a medieval French rabbi and author of a comprehensive commentary on the Talmud and commentary on the Tanach. Acclaimed for his ability to present the basic meaning of the text in a concise and lucid fashion, Rashi appeals to both learned scholars and beginning students, and his works remain a centerpiece of contemporary Jewish study.

first—barishonah—He created the heavens and the earth," for there is no "reishis" in the Torah that is not connected to the following word ... (Rashi)

This is what Rashi means. The verse quoted begins with the Hebrew word, "bereishis," which is translated as "in the beginning." As Rashi points out this word usually means "in the beginning" of something, such as of God's creating, which is not what the verse relates.

The proper Hebrew word to convey the meaning of the verse as it is generally understood, explains Rashi, is "barishonah," which means "at first." The fact that the Torah does not employ this word results in a remez, a hint, to another level of interpretation: b-reishis, which means "for the sake of reishis."[4] This would change the meaning of the verse to:

For the sake of "reishis" God made the heaven and the earth.

Rashi then brings other verses to show how the Hebrew word "reishis," or "first," is another name for both Torah and the Jewish people. As a result the verse, at least on the level of Remez, can be interpreted to mean:

---

[4] The Torah was dictated by God to Moshe Rabbeinu, letter-by-letter. If an "incorrect" word was used in a verse it was intentional and to allude to another level of explanation.

For the sake of Torah and/or the Jewish people, God made the heaven and the earth.

This idea, as Rashi also notes, is in fact true. God did not randomly make Creation but created everything as a way for the Torah to be fulfilled, and for the nation that would fulfill it. It is this that justifies all of existence, as the Talmud states:

Resh Lakish said: Why is it written, "And there was evening and there was morning, the sixth day" (Bereishis 1:31)? What is the reason for the additional Heh? (Shabbos 88a)

Resh Lakish's question arises because the Hebrew word for "sixth" in the verse begins with a letter Heh, the definite article: HEH-Shin-Shin-Yud. The numbers of the previous five days of Creation, however, are not preceded by the letter Heh, and Resh Lakish reveals why:

This teaches that The Holy One, Blessed is He, stipulated with the works of Creation and said: "If the Jewish people [in the future] accept the Torah, you will be able to continue to exist. If not, I will turn you back to null and void." (Shabbos 88a)

The null and void to which Resh Lakish refers is mentioned in the second verse of the Torah:

The land was null and void, and there was
darkness upon the face of the deep.
(Bereishis 1:2)

The Torah tells us that prior to the orderly
world with which we are familiar there was chaos.
This is was the starting point of Creation, and according to Resh Lakish, God was prepared to
make null and void the end point of Creation if the
Jewish people did not accept Torah when it was
offered to them. The question, is, how did Resh
Lakish arrive at his conclusion?

The letter Heh in gematria[5] corresponds to
the number five, an allusion to the five books of
the Torah: Bereishis, Shemos, Vayikra, Bamidbar,
and Devarim.[6] The number "six" exegetically alludes to the sixth day of Sivan in the year
2448/1313 BCE, when the Jewish people were
destined to accept Torah at Mt. Sinai. Thus, for the
sake of Torah and the nation destined to fulfill it,
the world was created.

The level of Drush, or exegesis, is more complicated. Whereas a hint can often be derived from
something that is visible, such as a misspelled
word or an extra letter, Drush may not be apparent on the surface and instead be based upon a
tradition.

---

[5] Jewish numerology based upon a long standing Kabbalah tradition.
[6] In English they are: Genesis, Exodus, Leviticus, Numbers, and
Deuteronomy respectively.

For example, the first word of the Torah, "bereishis," is spelled: Bais-Raish-Aleph-Shin-Yud-Tav. It can however be broken into two parts in the middle resulting in two words: "bara" and "shis," literally, "He created six."

Six what?

There is a discussion about the way in which God made Creation. One opinion says that He made all of Creation at the first moment when He said "Bereishis," and only had to put each element into its intended place on its particular day of Creation.[7] The other opinion says that all of the elements of Creation were not created at the first moment, but rather on their particular days.

The interpretation of "bara shis" seems to support the first opinion, that God made all aspects of Creation at the first moment. In fact, not just all the elements of the first six days, but of the six millennia that followed:

> This is the meaning of [the word] "Bereishis": bara shis, that [God created] the six millennia . . . (Sefer Igra d'Kallah 12a)

There is no hint in the verse to indicate this idea, especially since the word "shis" is the number six in Aramaic, not in Hebrew. The only way to authoritatively arrive at such a conclusion is to

---

[7] Rashi, Bereishis 1:14.

already have a tradition, a midrash[8] perhaps, that shows how the verse can be a source for the idea.

There are 13 different methods used for Drush according to the Sifra, and they are mentioned in the morning prayer service right before Pesukei D'Zimra, or the "Introductory Psalms." There are rules regarding when they can be applied and for what, but the main point is that such usage is usually based upon a long-standing Torah tradition that can be traced back to Moshe Rabbeinu.

The final level of Pardes is Sod, or "Secret." This refers to the mystical level of Torah, otherwise known as Kabbalah. The word "Kabbalah" actually means "received," because like the rest of the Oral Tradition, Sod is an area of Torah learning that has been passed down from generation to generation, going back to when Torah was first given.

For some, Kabbalah is controversial. As mentioned, it is an area of Torah learning that belongs to Torah Sh'b'al Peh, the Oral Tradition meant to accompany and explain the Written Law. People tend to think, and often rightly so, that oral traditions are less reliable than written traditions.

In addition, since Kabbalah, for a long period of time, was only known to a handful of Torah leaders and students, its seemingly sudden emer-

---

[8] The basis of this word "midrash" is "drush," and it is usually some story or account that may or may not be true. Regardless midrashim, of which there are many, are usually a method for teaching principles of the Oral Law.

gence onto the mainstream Torah scene, 1500 years after Mt. Sinai, was suspicious. It also does not help that Kabbalah contains many ideas that, at least on the surface, seem somewhat different from the more revealed areas of Torah learning.

In response to this controversy a great and well-known sixteenth century Kabbalist, Rabbi Moshe Cordevero,[9] otherwise known as the "Ramak," wrote:

> Now that the wisdom of the "Truth"[10] has become revealed and made known among Jewish scholars—an inheritance for the "Assembly of Ya'akov" through Moshe Rabbeinu from God—anyone who denies it or argues with it is a heretic, because he denies a portion of Torah Sh'b'al Peh. He removes himself from the "Faithful of the Jewish people." From the time that it became well-known among the Jewish people, that is from the time of the Ramban[11] onward . . . Previous to this time it was hidden and revealed only to a few fitting people in each generation, as it is known in the responsa of the Geonim.[12] In the time of the Ramban however, it became known among the Jewish people, and not a single scholar from all the wise of the Jewish

---

[9] Tzfas, 1522–1570.
[10] Another name for Kabbalah.
[11] Rabbi Moshe ben Nachman, otherwise known as "Nachmanides," who lived between 1194–1270.
[12] 589 - 1038 CE.

people from whose "waters" we drink when learning their commentaries on Talmud and legal decisions, have argued against it. (Pardes, Sha'ar Eser V'Lo Teisha, Ch. 9)

There were basically two major turning points in the history of Kabbalah. The first occurred during the time of Rabbi Shimon bar Yochai, otherwise known as the "Rashbi."[13] It was the Rashbi, on the day of his death around 120 CE, who revealed the tradition of Kabbalah he had received from his teachers to nine of his students. It was their manuscripts that were published as the "Zohar" in the 13th century.[14]

The second major turning point was the life of the Arizal, or Rabbi Yitzchak Luria. He lived in the 16th century, from 1534–1572, and explained the Zohar in ways that no one had since it was first revealed. He also dealt with many other Kabbalistic matters, but his main work, "Aitz Chaim," reveals many of the details regarding Creation up until the first verse in the Torah, often thought to be off limits.[15]

---

[13] The name is derived by combining the initials of each of the Hebrew words, "Rabbi Shimon bar Yochai."

[14] The Zohar was only published for the first time by Rabbi Moses de León in 1240 CE in France.

[15] Chagigah 11b. Even though the Arizal lived long after the Rashbi he is considered to be one of the foremost authorities on Kabbalah until today. Though he died young his level of scholarship was recognized by the Torah authorities of the time, and ever since. He is often universally referred to as "The Teacher."

In a manner of speaking, Kabbalah is to the rest of Torah what Quantum Physics is to college physics. Even though both originate from the same source and explain the same Creation, Quantum Physics is considerably more technical and significantly more complicated and abstract than physics on a college level.

Likewise, the Kabbalah of Aitz Chaim is extremely abstract, possesses a language of its own, and is very technical. It is very different even from the parts of the Zohar that only provide a more Kabbalistic approach to the weekly Torah reading. It can take an entire lifetime to understand Kabbalah on this level, and then some.

The primary focus of this aspect of Kabbalah is the sefiros and partzufim. Completely spiritual, they comprise the system which God employed to make and maintain Creation. Essentially, they filter the light of God to the point that it can actually result in creations, including man.

At its Source, the light of God, referred to as "Ohr Ain Sof," the "Light Without Limit," or the "Infinite Light," is far too spiritually intense for anything else to exist. To continually make Creation possible the Ohr Ain Sof must be reduced, filtered so-to-speak, and the sefiros, of which there are 10, and partzufim, of which in general there are usually five, are the mechanisms by which this occurs.

The sefiros will be discussed in more detail in a later session. In the meantime, the Kabbalistic interpretation of the verse of the Torah is as follows:

> [The sefirah of] Binah[16] created the six "points"[17] [of Chesed, Gevurah, Tifferes, Netzach, Hod, and Yesod]. (Biur HaGR"A, Sifra d'Tzniusa, Ch. 1)

This means that the sefiros of Chesed through Yesod were the basis of the six days of Creation. Each contained the spiritual potential to bring into existence what was created on its respective day.

Not only were the sefiros of Chesed through Yesod the basis of the six days of Creation, they were also the basis of the corresponding millennia:

> Each day of Creation alludes to a thousand years of our existence, and every little detail that occurred on these days will have its corresponding event happen at the proportionate time during its millennium. (Biur HaGR"A, Sifra d'Tzniusa, Ch. 5)

This will be easier to appreciate in the session about the sefiros. In the meantime, this has been an example of how a single verse from the Torah can be explained on four different levels of under-

---

[16] The name means "Understanding," and it is the third highest sefirah.
[17] Nekudos in Hebrew.

standing. In fact, these four levels of Torah explanation correspond to the four main areas of Torah learning.

The most basic area of Torah learning is the written verse itself—Mikrah, which can be read, for the most part, without explanation. After that is Mishnah, the concise legal teachings that comprise the body of Torah Sh'b'al Peh—the Oral Law. They were received together with the Written Law at Mt. Sinai, which cannot be fully understood in detail without its companion, the Oral Law.

Originally the teachings of the Mishnah were memorized and discussed on an ongoing basis in the Bais Midrash, Torah

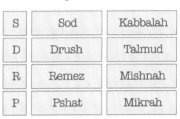

S	Sod	Kabbalah
D	Drush	Talmud
R	Remez	Mishnah
P	Pshat	Mikrah

Pardes & The Four Areas of Torah Learning

study halls, to ensure continuity and accuracy. When persecution of Jews, especially Torah scholars, became intense during Roman times and threatened the ongoing accurate transmission of the Oral Law, it was codified and redacted. This occurred in 186 CE under the guidance of Rabbi Yehudah HaNasi.

To maintain the integrity of the Oral Law the Mishnah was recorded as terse and often incomplete statements. They are, for the most part, memory devices meant to assist those who have taken the time to learn the complete laws from a competent Torah educator. They hint to information by what they say, don't say, or how they say what they do, and therefore correspond to the level of Remez.

The Talmud, learned in most yeshivos over the centuries, is the level of Drush. It was not recorded until 499 CE when the Mishnah alone was no longer sufficient to ensure the veracity of the transmission of the Oral Law. The Jewish people not only suffered ongoing persecution, but exile and dispersion as well. This necessitated the recording of the discussions and explanations meant to be triggered by the Mishnah.

The Talmud also contains many non-legal discussions called "aggadata," which are basically Talmudic midrashim. Most midrashim, also part of the Oral Tradition, are found outside of the Talmud in a collection of independent volumes. They often provide background information and details of stories in the Torah, or lessons about life.

The last and most sublime area of Torah learning is Kabbalah, introduced to the world in the Zohar and expanded upon in the teachings of the Arizal, and many other Kabbalists since. As mentioned earlier, it is to this level of Torah learning that the topic of reincarnation belongs.

two
what are the sefiros?

WHEN MOSHE RABBEINU was on Mt. Sinai, after he pleaded with God to forgive the Jewish people for the sin of the golden calf, he made an additional request:

> [Moshe] said [to God], "Show me now Your glory!" (Shemos 33:18)

The request is understandable. It is God's response that requires explanation:

> He said, "You will not be able to see My face, for man shall not see Me and live." And God said: "Behold, there is a place with Me, and you shall stand on the rock. And it shall be that when My glory passes by, I will place you

into the cleft of the rock, and I will cover you with My hand until I have passed by. Then I will remove My hand, and you will see My back but My face shall not be seen." (Shemos 33:20-23)

If taken at face value the story reads fine. One question however changes everything: If God is non-corporeal then what is His face, His hand, and His back? Why does seeing His face result in death?

The answer to this question is the basis of all of Kabbalah. It is the greatest mystery of life, the solving of which can take lifetimes. The insights that emerge from doing so however greatly enhance one's understanding and appreciation of life, and lead directly to a discussion about the sefiros.

Physical intensity is both discernible and quantifiable. Over exposure to the sun can result in sunburn, and over time, skin cancer. Over exposure to radiation can be equally deadly, if not more so, and receiving too much information in a short while can cause a person to mentally "shut down." People who are "too intense" may have a difficult time making and keeping friends.

Sometimes intensity is an inevitable part of a system. For example, a hydroelectric plant must produce tremendous amounts of energy if it is to supply electricity to tens of millions of customers on a continuous basis. At the source the energy is too intense for personal use and it would be very destructive.

The same is true of God's light, only more so. The spiritual intensity of God's light at its source is so intense that it precludes the existence of anything physical, or anything else for that matter. It is called "Ohr Ain Sof," or the "Light Without End," and there is nothing in life to which it can be compared.

With respect to electricity a system had to be devised to step down the intensity of the current so that it will not destroy that with which it comes in contact. The idea was that by the time the electrical current reaches a community it is weak enough to be used in a constructive manner.

Unlike electricity though, God's Divine current is unaffected by impediments such as friction. Unimpeded the Ohr Ain Sof goes on infinitely without weakening in the slightest. To be "stepped down," especially enough to result in physical Creation, and eventually a free will being, God wills it, continuously. This is the Kabbalistic idea of "tzimtzum," or "constriction."

The system which God created to function in this way is comprised of 10 sefiros. The name itself means "counting" since each sefirah is a particular measure of Divine light. Hence they are also called "middos," which means "measures," or "traits," which are the measure of a someone or something.

The 10 sefiros are: Keser, Chochmah, Binah, Chesed, Gevurah, Tifferes, Netzach, Hod, Yesod, and Malchus. Translated, they are: Crown, Wisdom, Understanding, Kindness, Strength, Beauty, Eternity, Glory, Foundation, and Kingdom.

A sefirah has the capacity to receive Divine light and hold back or "filter" higher, more spiritual levels of light. This results in the descending of a lesser, more "physical" level of light, and a lower level of sefirah.

For example, the highest level of sefirah is "Keser," or "Crown," because it "sits" on top of the lower nine sefiros like a crown. It retains an extremely intense level of light and what descends after results in the next level of sefirah called "Chochmah," or "Wisdom."

The name itself indicates the point of the transformation. By descending from the level of Keser to Chochmah the Ohr Ain Sof becomes more "tangible." However, it is still quite abstract and, therefore, this level is considered to be completely spiritual.

The level of Binah, which means "understanding," is the level on which the light has become physical enough to create something mater-

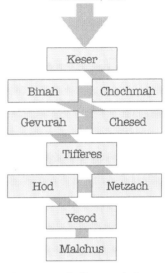

The Ohr Ain Sof enters the "Challal" and creates the first sefirah of "Keser" before being filtered and descending to create the level of "Chochmah," etc.

Diagrammatic Representation of The Ten Sefiros

ial. Therefore, descending from Chochmah to Binah is called "Yaish m'Ayin," or "Something from Nothing," since physicality has finally "emerged" from spiritual light, making it discernible by man.

The next level of sefirah is called "Chesed," or "Kindness." It says, "A world of Chesed You created" (Tehillim 89:3), which has been explained in many ways. A Kabbalistic interpretation is that it refers to the creation of the sefirah of Chesed by the sefirah of Binah, as it says:

> [The sefirah of] Binah created the six "points"[1] [of Chesed, Gevurah, Tifferes, Netzach, Hod, and Yesod]. (Biur HaGR"A, Sifra d'Tzniusa, Ch. 1)

It is called a "world of Chesed" because this also marked the beginning of physical Creation, since Chesed corresponds to the first one thousand years of human history. Creation was a function of God's kindness and is supposed to be the forum for human kindness, as Avraham Avinu tried to teach the world:

> Avraham caused the Name of The Holy One, Blessed is He, to be uttered by the mouth of every passerby. How? After [travelers] had eaten and drunk [their fill], they stood up to bless him. He said to them however, "Did you eat of mine? You ate of that which belongs to

---

[1] Nekudos in Hebrew.

the God of the Universe. Thank, praise and bless Him Who spoke and the world came into being." (Sotah 10b)

Chesed can only emerge from binah—understanding. First Avraham searched for the bottom line of life:

Rebi Yitzchak began: "Listen, O daughter, and look, and incline your ear; and forget your nation and your father's house" (Tehillim 45:11). Rebi Yitzchak said, "This may be compared to one who was traveling from place to place when he saw a burning mansion. He said, 'Is it possible that this mansion is without someone responsible?'[2] The owner of the mansion looked out at him and said, 'I am the owner of the mansion.'[3] So too Avraham Avinu said, 'Is it possible that the world is without someone responsible for it?' God 'looked out' at him and said, 'I am the Master of the world.' " (Bereishis Rabbah 39:1)

Once Avraham understood that God was still running the world, and that life is the result of His kindness, he modeled himself similarly. As a re-

---

[2] Seeing the mansion burning he thought that it had been abandoned. Likewise, the evil in the world could make one believe that God has abandoned His world.
[3] That is, I am the owner of the mansion, and I was the one who lit the fire

sult, he became the representation of Chesed in history.

Gevurah comes after Chesed. It means "strength" and implies constriction and discipline. Whereas Chesed represents the emanation and spreading of Divine light, Gevurah is about the opposite, which raises the question: How can a light of constriction evolve from a light of emanation?

The answer has to do with the nature of Chesed itself. Kindness is not only about giving, but about holding back as well. The point of Chesed is to allow the recipient to become more independent, not less. This is why the greatest form of tzedakah is not simply giving a person in need a free handout. It is giving him the opportunity to earn his own livelihood.[4]

Therefore, inherent in Chesed is restraint. Just as God is thoughtful about what, to whom, and when He gives, a person must likewise be disciplined in his acts of lovingkindness to others. He must not simply give to discharge his obligation to help others, but give to help the other person to improve his quality of life.

Such balanced giving is the level of Tifferes, the next sefirah. It is "beauty" and "harmony" because it represents the perfect emulation of God. It is the balance between two extremes, Chesed and Gevurah, just as Ya'akov Avinu was the balance between Avraham, who represented Chesed, and Yitzchak, who represented Gevurah.

---

[4] Yad Chazakah, Hilchos Matanos Aniyim, Ch. 10:7.

As such Tifferes, like Ya'akov Avinu, also represents Torah in general, which was given to man to help him emulate God. Torah is what allows a person to guide his life according to the priorities of his soul, the eternal aspect of man which is destined for the World-to-Come. Therefore, from Tifferes emerges the sefirah of Netzach, which means "eternity."

The eighth sefirah is Hod, which is Glory. When Moshe Rabbeinu descended the mountain after achieving atonement for the Jewish people for their involvement in the sin of the golden calf, he emitted karnei hod—beams of glory.[5] He received these when God caused His Presence to pass by Moshe Rabbeinu as he remained shielded by a cleft in the rock.

Essentially these "beams" of light were his soul radiating out through his skin to the outside world. The closeness to God that Moshe achieved at that time so elevated him that he became part angel,[6] and his skin, less physical. The glory of his soul was allowed to penetrate to the outside and be seen by others, which was an overwhelming experience for all those who saw him.[7]

At this point a person becomes completely righteous, and arrives at the level of Yesod. They have made their will like God's will,[8] and become the conduit for the light of God to the life-sustain-

---

[5] Shemos 34:29.
[6] Devarim Rabbah 11:14.
[7] Shemos 34:30.
[8] Pirkei Avos 2:4.

ing benefit of the rest of mankind.[9] This is what the verse means when it says that the "righteous person is the foundation—yesod—of the world" (Mishlei 10:25).

This is also why it was Yosef HaTzaddik who fed Egypt and his family during famine.[10] The sefirah of Yesod, represented by Yosef, is the one through which the blessing of God flows into the world.

The tenth and last sefirah is that of Malchus, or Kingdom. Malchus is pure synergy, a perfection that is achieved by binding together all of the various different pieces into a unified whole that is far greater than the sum of its parts. It is what emerges when the light has passed through the previous nine sefiros. It is what is achieved when a person has taken these lessons to heart and applied their messages to life.

Worlds & Partzufim

The 10 sefiros are the backbone of all of Creation. Kabbalah explains that they are divided up into five levels, into five "worlds," or "partzufim."[11] In general, one sefirah corresponds to one world, the only exception being the world of Yetzirah which corresponds to the six sefiros of Chesed, Gevurah, Tifferes, Netzach, Hod, and Yesod.

---

[9] Brochos 17b.

[10] Bereishis, Ch. 42.

[11] A partzuf is a face, which tends to reveal to the outside what a person is feeling on the inside. Likewise, when a sefirah is viewed as a unit of 10 sefiros, its "inside" is being revealed to the outside.

How does a single sefirah become an entire world of its own? In a similar manner that a person goes from being only a member of one family to being the head of his own family.

	Keser	Adam Kad.
S	Chochmah	Atzilus
D	Binah	Beriyah
R	Ches-Yesod	Yetzirah
P	Malchus	Asiyah

The 10 Sefiros & Five Worlds

As a child, a person is only a single family member of his entire family. In this respect he is like a single sefirah from the "family" of 10 sefiros. After growing up, getting married, and having children of his own, he becomes the head of his own family, comparable to becoming a world, or a partzuf in his own right.

The highest level of world is Adam Kadmon, literally "First Man," which is the sefirah of Keser with 10 sefiros of its own. The names of the 10 sefiros are exactly the same as the names of the general 10 sefiros. Since the overall level of sefirah is Keser, each of its 10 sefiros are aspects of it, the first one being Keser of Keser, the second being Chochmah of Keser, and so on.

Using the same analogy, though a single member of a family is unique, he or she also shares traits common with others in the family, especially the parents. Nevertheless, each person will exhibit the trait that is unique to him or her since it will be impacted by the general overall nature of the person. Likewise, for example, the Chochmah of Keser will be different somewhat from the general level of Chochmah since it is a part of Keser.

The next world down is Atzilus, Emanations, which is the sefirah of Chochmah with 10 sefiros of its own. It is unlike Adam Kadmon because it is well-defined, but it is also unlike the worlds that follow since it is completely Godly and spiritual.

Atzilus is followed by the world of Beriyah, or Creation, which corresponds to the sefirah of Binah. As mentioned earlier Atzilus is the level of "Ayin," or "nothing," and Binah, or Beriyah, is the level of "Yaish," or "something" since this is the level on which physical Creation comes into being.

Yetzirah, or Formation, is next. Beriyah is creation ex nihilo, whereas yetzirah is more the manipulation of what already physically exists. This level corresponds to the six sefiros of Chesed through Yesod, which are the basis of the six days of Creation. As the commentators explain, all of Creation came into being at the first moment. It was over the next six days that each element was completed and put into its Divinely-intended place.

The final world or level of consciousness is called "Asiyah," which means "action." It corresponds to the sefirah of Malchus and the physical world in which our universe exists and in which we act out our lives.

Keser, Chochmah, and Binah from the beginning of Creation had all 10 of their sefiros. Chesed through Yesod each only had six of their 10 sefiros. Malchus, however, had almost nothing in order to allow man, though his deeds, to draw down the Ohr Ain Sof and become a partner with God in the perfection of Creation.[12]

All of this, however, represents only half of the story. It is called in Kabbalah, a "yeridah tzorech aliyah," a "going down for the sake of going up." To fulfill the purpose of Creation the Ohr Ain Sof had to first move away from its Source and become less spiritual as it continued to descend. Consequently, the light became less Godly as well.

The result is a world that not only supports the concept of free will, it even allows a person to reject God. The light has become so filtered that even heresy is possible, which is surprising considering that everything is made and sustained by the Ohr Ain Sof at all times.

The challenge of life, therefore, is to reverse the trend. It is to climb the "ladder" of Divine light in pursuit of its Source, God Himself. As the next session will explain, this process is one and the same as self-discovery, because to ascend from sefirah to sefirah is to also ascend from one level of soul to another.

---

[12] Shabbos 119b.

three
five levels of
soul

WHAT MAKES ONE person more spiritual
than another? Everyone has a soul, so why isn't
one person just as spiritual as the next? Why do
some people choose religion while others choose
agnosticism, or even atheism, and with what
seems to be a clear conscience?

Without question knowledge plays a major
role in such a decision, but not the only one. Two
people can know the exact same information and
still go in opposite ideological directions. There are
scientists who believe in God and some who do
not, and both camps are intelligent and well-informed.

Emotions also play a role in such decisions. A
person can be intelligent and well-informed but
emotionally insecure. For such a person "religion"

might be a form of emotional security, whereas for more secure people it might represent an escape from the harsher realities of daily life.

The question is, what about people who are intelligent, well-informed, and emotionally stable, and religious as well? They follow God specifically because they have made a well-informed and balanced decision. Why haven't the other intelligent, well-informed, and emotionally stable people made a similar choice?

The answer to this question has to do with levels of soul. Everyone has a soul, but not everyone has access to all of its levels, or even most of them. This is what allows people, scientists included, to walk around and not even believe they have a soul, let alone levels of it.

The first chapter of Sha'ar HaGilgulim begins with the following statement:

> We begin with what Chazal[1] have written, that the soul has five names. Their order, from bottom to top, is: Nefesh, Ruach, Neshamah, Chayah, and Yechidah. Undoubtedly, they are not called these [names] by chance. (Sha'ar HaGilgulim, Introduction 1)

It is not that the soul has five names, but that it has five parts, each with its own name. The

---

[1] This is spelled: Ches-Zayin-Lamed, and stands for, "Chachomeinu, zichronum l'vrochah," "our wise ones, may they be remembered for blessing."

highest level of the soul is called "Yechidah," which means "unit" because everything is extremely unified on this level. It is a level of soul so close to its Source, the Ohr Ain Sof,[2] that it always maintains its sublime unity and mystery.

The Five Levels of Soul

After the light has been "filtered" the next level of soul down is called "Chayah," which means "life." This is the level of soul that is considered to be the "source" of life for the levels that follow it, even though it receives its light from Yechidah. It is often referred to as the "soul within the soul."

The next level of soul is called, "Neshamah," which comes from the word "neshimah," which means "breath." It is as if the light of this level of soul is a "breath" that is "blown" downward creating a "breeze" of light, or the level of soul called, "Ruach." This "breath" of light finally comes to a halt on the level of the body as the level of soul called, "Nefesh," which means "rest."

The Torah says:

> For the Nefesh of the flesh is in the blood, and I have therefore given it to you [to be placed] upon the altar, to atone for your souls. For it is the blood that atones for the soul. (Vayikra 17:11)

---

[2] The Infinite Light of God.

The Nefesh acts as the interface between the spiritual and physical components of man. The blood may be the life force of the body, but the Nefesh is the life source of the blood, through which it miraculously passes the Divine light it receives to the body. It is to this that the Talmud alludes when it explains:

> Our Rabbis taught: There are three partners in [the creation of] man: The Holy One, Blessed is He, his father, and his mother. His father supplies the seed of the white substance out of which are formed the child's bones, sinews, nails, the brain in his head and the white in his eye. His mother supplies the seed of the red substance out of which is formed his skin, flesh, hair, blood and the black of his eye. The Holy One, Blessed is He, gives him the spirit and the breath, beauty of features, eyesight, the power of hearing and the ability to speak and to walk, understanding and discernment. When his time to depart from the world approaches, The Holy One, Blessed is He, takes away His share and leaves the shares of his father and his mother with him. (Niddah 31a)

Without a Nefesh the blood can no longer keep the body alive, and the person passes from this world. As the soul is withdrawn and ascends, the body remains behind for burial.

Not only are there five levels of soul, but each of the five levels has the same five levels of its own, subsets of the five levels of soul. For example, there is a Nefesh of the Nefesh, a Ruach of the Nefesh, a Neshamah of the Nefesh, etc.

	Yechidah
	Chayah
Nefesh	Neshamah
	Ruach
	Nefesh

The Five Levels of Nefesh

Likewise, the subsets themselves also have their own five levels of soul, subsets of the subsets, etc., resulting in a Nefesh of the Nefesh of the Nefesh, a Ruach of the Nefesh of the Nefesh, etc. The splintering of soul levels continues from level to level, the souls of the next level being smaller and less spiritual than those of the previous level.

Therefore even within a single level of soul there are countless levels. The higher the level of soul a person is able to access the more Divine light will reach and impact his body and therefore his level of spirituality. This is the single most important factor in determining a person's spiritual level, regardless of how intelligent, well-informed, or emotionally stable he or she may be.

All levels exist in every human soul, making it only an issue of to which level of soul a person will gain access. The same way a computer program may display many functions but only allow access to some,[3] likewise all levels of soul though

---

[3] To entice users to purchase their programs.

"available" are not necessarily "accessible" without tikun, or personal rectification.

To appreciate the path to personal tikun it is important to understand that there is a direct correlation between the five levels of soul and the four levels of Pardes.[4] There is no level of Torah learning that corresponds to the level of Yechidah because of its sublime unity. On this level knowledge is something that is experienced, not learned.

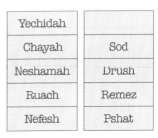

Yechidah	
Chayah	Sod
Neshamah	Drush
Ruach	Remez
Nefesh	Pshat

Correlation Between Levels of Soul & Levels of Pardes

This teaches that advancement in Torah learning results in access to higher levels of soul. As a person ascends from the level of Pshat to Remez, to Drush, and finally to Sod, he should, theoretically,[5] be able to systematically access the levels of Ruach, Neshamah, and Chayah respectively. At the very least the person increases his or her level of spiritual sensitivity, allowing him or her to live more like a soul than a body.[6]

---

[4] The four levels of Torah learning. See Session #1.

[5] Spiritual growth involves two parts: 1.) additional knowledge and, 2.) the integration of the new knowledge (often referred to as "Haskel," or "Discernment). Just the learning of new ideas is not enough to cause a person to move up notches on the spiritual ladder.

[6] Materialism attracts the body, and it is willing to sacrifice long term spiritual gain for short term physical pleasure. The opposite is true of the soul, which is why spiritually-inclined people tend to be able to be self-sacrificing for higher causes.

In essence, this is the process of teshuvah—repentance. The Talmud says:

> A person only sins when a spirit of insanity enters him. (Sotah 3a)

Sanity can be defined as being "in touch" with reality, as acting in a way that rationally "fits" the given set of circumstances. The assumption is that a person wants to act rationally and if he does not it is because he misperceives his situation, either accidentally or because of some mental incapacitation. The former can be corrected but the latter may be the result of a permanent mental disability.

Sanity is not all-or-nothing though. Decisions are based upon perceptions which in turn are based upon assumptions about life. There is an objective reality but a person's perception of it can be very subjective, based upon the assumptions that society as a whole and individuals in particular have accepted as true.

For example, even an atheist lacks proof that God does not exist. Instead, lacking what he assumes to be sufficient proof that God does exist, he perceives that He is merely a concept, and a mistaken one at that. He assumes that if God existed he would be able to perceive Him, and that it can be no other way.

This is even though atheists rarely, if ever, thoroughly investigates why others do believe in God. They take for granted, for one reason or another, that there is information they have ignored or overlooked, about Who God is and how He runs His world. Information that could, and more than likely would, change their perception about their Creator. It has happened to many a atheist in the past.

There is even an expression for this phenomenon: "There are no atheists in a foxhole." It means that when confronted with the possibility of death, or even just extreme danger, many people who previously ignored God suddenly turn to Him for help. The danger together with the realization of personal limitation pushes such people to consider the possibility of a higher, more powerful being that can help them in ways they cannot help themselves.

Why does a sense of imminent danger cause such people to change their spiritual tune? It is because danger humbles the body, neutralizing it to a large degree, silencing it. This is when the soul finally gets an opportunity to "speak," elevating the person spiritually in manner that is supposed happen through education, and without danger.

To appreciate how this is supposed to happen it is important to first become aware of an insightful statement in the Talmud:

> There is no time in which a man enjoys greater happiness than in those days [in the womb] . . . [He] is also taught the entire Torah from beginning to end . . . (Niddah 30b)

If it is true that a baby knows the entire Torah prior to birth, why is it that he recalls none of it after he is born? This is because, as the Talmud explains, the angel who taught him Torah causes him to forget what he previously learned, and he is therefore born with no knowledge of his previous education.

No knowledge, that is, on a conscious level. The knowledge remains with a child even after birth. This means that education is not about learning new ideas but a matter of remembering old ones. The learning on the "outside" helps to bring the internal knowledge to the conscious mind where it is "remembered." The deeper the level of learning that a person does, the deeper the recovery of knowledge will be, and the more spiritually sensitive the person will become.

As a result of becoming in touch with higher levels of soul, the person's assumptions about life will become altered and with them, his perceptions about life. His priorities will likewise change, reflected in a changed lifestyle. He will become more spiritual and will have done teshuvah.

On the surface it may appear as if the person has just become wiser and more spiritual. In actuality he has accessed higher levels of soul and Divine light, and this in turn spiritually elevates his body. As the process continues, body and soul will become increasingly more unified, and the person will feel increasingly more complete and at peace.

This is the answer to the original question. People draw different conclusions about God and the validity of Torah based upon the level of soul to which they have access. The higher the level of soul they are accessing the more spiritually sensitive they will become. Their assumptions about life will become more objective, and their perception of God will become clearer. The process of gaining access to higher levels of soul therefore is a function of Torah learning.

four
what is an adam shalaim?

LITERALLY, "ADAM SHALAIM" means "complete person," the term used in Sha'ar HaGilgulim to refer to a person who has fulfilled his spiritual potential.[1] The Torah says that man was made in the "image of God," and when a person lives up this image then he has earned the title, "Adam Shalaim."

The process to reach this level is mentioned at the beginning of Sha'ar HaGilgulim:

> A person does not acquire all of [levels of soul] at once, but rather, [he acquires each level] based upon his merits. At first he acquires the lowest of them all called "Nefesh."

---

[1] Sha'ar HaGilgulim, Introduction 18.

After that, if he merits more, he also acquires Ruach, just as it is explained in many places in the Zohar, such as in Parashas Vayechi, Parashas Terumah, and especially at the beginning of Parashas Mishpatim (94b), where it says: "Come and see: When a person is born, they give him a Nefesh, etc." (Sha'ar HaGilgulim, Introduction 1)

An Adam Shalaim is someone who has acquired all three levels of soul: Nefesh, Ruach, and Neshamah. Though most people barely acquire the lower levels of Nefesh, it says in Sha'ar HaGilgulim, the potential exists for a person to access all three levels of soul, and in general he will reincarnate until he does or history runs out.

It works similarly to receiving a promotion in the business world. Very often a person starts a job on a relatively basic level, but if he does his job well and shows potential to work on a higher level he will be noticed by Management and merit to be promoted. Consequently, his status will change and his resources to do his higher level of job will be increased.

If he does his new job well and continues to show ambition he will merit to be promoted again, and this will continue until he can no longer reach a higher level of employment. As he climbs the corporate ladder he will become more resourceful, more competent, and even more confident. He will feel an increased sense of fulfillment with each promotion, since he will be using more of his potential.

When a person first comes into the world he barely has the level of Nefesh. It is all he needs because all that a baby must do is survive from day to day, in order to reach his next stage of life. Completely dependent upon others, it just requires its bodily functions to work properly, and his Nefesh is enough to do this, and then some:

> When a person is born and emerges into the "air of this world," his Nefesh enters him. If his actions are appropriate, he will merit his Ruach which will enter him at the completion of his thirteenth year when he is called a "complete person," as it is known. If henceforth his actions are again appropriate, then his Neshamah will enter him at the completion of his twentieth year, as mentioned in Sabba of Mishpatim. (Sha'ar HaGilgulim, Introduction 2)

In this case "complete person" is not the translation of "Adam Shalaim," but of "Ish Gamur," an intermediate stage of completion. It is a person who has successfully acquired all levels of Nefesh relevant to him.[2] This includes the five levels of Nefesh: Nefesh of Nefesh, Ruach of Nefesh, Neshamah of Nefesh, Chayah of Nefesh, and the Yechidah of Nefesh.

Apparently the level of Nefesh is sufficient for a person to do what he must for the first 13 years of his life. Even though a person matures significantly during his first 13 years, achieving a remarkable level of independence and self-reliance, he does this without the level of Ruach, which he cannot receive until 13 years, and even that is only if the person has merited to receive his Ruach.

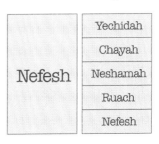

Nefesh	Yechidah
	Chayah
	Neshamah
	Ruach
	Nefesh

The Five Levels Of Nefesh

To appreciate the difference receiving one's Ruach makes to spiritual growth, it is important to know another correlation, between the levels of soul and the process that leads to action. Even though

Yechidah	Ratzon
Chayah	Hirhur
Neshamah	Machshavah
Ruach	Dibur
Nefesh	Ma'aseh

Correlation Between Levels of Soul & Action

---

[2] In the first introduction of Sha'ar HaGilgulim it is explained how a person does not have to acquire every level of the Nefesh, but only those levels relevant to the one from which his soul has come, but on each of the five levels of Nefesh. For example, if the person's soul came from the Malchus of the Nefesh of the Nefesh, he need only acquire the Malchus of the Ruach of the Nefesh to be considered to have rectified the entire level of the Ruach of the Nefesh, and ready to work on acquiring the level of the Neshamah of the Nefesh, etc.

many actions seem to occur unconsciously, there is actually a "chain of command" connecting up a person's will with the actual act.

This is easier to understand through an example, such as a person who becomes inspired to make a donation. This is the level of "Ratzon," or of unconscious will, and therefore it is very unlikely that the person will even be aware of this inspiration at this point. While he goes about his life as usual, this inspiration will move in the direction of more concrete and more conscious thought.

Then it begins to occur to him, also somewhat unconsciously, where he might make a donation. This is the level of "Hirhur," which is more like whimsical thinking.

When the person starts to consciously consider a place to give his donation, he is working on the level of "Machshavah," which means "thought." As he mentally comes to a conclusion about the intended destination of his donation, he may speak about it as part of the process of setting it in motion. This is called "Dibur," or "Speech."

The last level in the action chain-of-command is "Ma'aseh," which means "Action." This is the level on which the benefactor goes through the motions of completing his original will, writing the check and delivering it to the recipient. Having done this, the person will feel as if his has been fulfilled.

This process goes on all the time throughout the course of people's lives. However, very often they have no idea why they do what they do because their will remains hidden from them all the way to the final level of Ma'aseh. They act somewhat mindlessly, making it easier to make errors in judgment that can even result in tragedy, God forbid.

Accessing the level of Ruach allows a person to "intercept" his will on a higher level, before it reaches the level of action. He can discuss it and better evaluate what he has been inspired to do, making it less likely that he will err. He will be able to articulate his thoughts, allowing him to become more conscious of them and therefore, more in control of them.

Should a person rectify the level of Ruach and gain access to his level of Neshamah, the same thing will be true on an even higher level. He will gain the ability to know his will on the level of Machshavah, resulting in greater self-knowledge and personal control.

There is another way to look at the improvement in the spiritual quality of life when a person acquires a higher level of soul, evident by the way people act and speak.

While some people act in a base manner others act in a more refined way. While the actions of the former are more "animalistic" in nature, those of the latter seem more sophisticated, more "human," or actually, more Divine. We know what levels people are capable of living up to, and when they don't we are disappointed. When they do, we are impressed.

It is easy to act instinctually. It is far more difficult to act consciously and according to a high standard. It takes will and a lot of effort, something that people to do not expend unless they see the value in doing so. The more they understand and appreciate the importance of living in the image of God, the more effort they will make to do so and the more refined their actions will become.

This is the entire point of education, in particular, Torah education. The knowledge is to help a person understand why it is personally meaningful to spiritually refine one's actions. The mitzvos, particularly those which are action-oriented, provide the real-time training. Combined, a person is able to master the level of Nefesh.

Although society has coined phrases such as, "Actions speak louder than words," this is only true in some respects. Animals can be trained to perform relatively sophisticated and refined actions, so how much more so human beings. Refined actions are not necessarily proof of a refined personality.

Though people can also be trained to speak in a sophisticated manner, it is less likely that this will occur, and more likely that at some point, their manner of speech will betray them. More than action speech is a matter of level of intelligence and spiritual sophistication. As the Zohar says, a person is measured by what he or she says.[3] We are, in many ways, what we speak.

This is not just a matter of politeness. A per-

---

[3] Zohar, Balak 193b.

son who has acquired the level of Ruach is one for whom speech is holy. He will not abuse speech and certainly not defile it with improper language. Furthermore, he will not waste time with idle chatter or discuss things of little importance.

On such a spiritual level a person does not have that much difficulty in abstaining from base actions. His struggle will be to perfect the way he speaks, avoiding sins such as derogatory speech about others, called "loshon hara." Or, it might be to pray more clearly and with more patience.

The level up from Ruach is Neshamah. This corresponds to the level of Machshavah, or conscious thought. Everyone thinks, but not always so consciously, which is why so much of what they say and do is quite automatic, which can be costly, if not in this world then in the World-to-Come.

When a person is a conscious thinker then he not only thinks before he acts or speaks, he also has self-awareness. He can see the way he acts and is able to evaluate himself. This allows for greater self-perfection and fulfillment, because he can constantly tweak his approach to life.

On such a level a person is already in control of his actions and the way he speaks. If he sins it is only on the level of thought, and not as the average person might who daily has illicit thoughts. On such a level, their sins might be not thinking Torah thoughts when they should, or thinking them when they shouldn't.

A sin on the level of Machshavah might be thinking about important matters at times they shouldn't, such as during Shemonah Esrai. Or, perhaps it just thinking something derogatory about a person that they would never articulate.

There are people who currently live on such levels, or close to them. To meet such people can be an overwhelming spiritual experience because their soul is able to project itself to the outside world. It can spiritually overwhelming for others not on such a level, as it was for the rest of the nation when Moshe Rabbeinu descended Mt. Sinai exuding beams of light.[4]

Not everyone understands what they experience in the presence of such people. They do however admit to experiencing something powerful. It is very uplifting to interact with an Adam Shalaim, someone who lives in the image of God. It is also relatively rare, but something everyone must strive to achieve. If you do not reach for the stars it is difficult to leave the mud.

---

[4] Shemos 34:30.

five
what is reincarnation?

THE HEBREW WORD for "reincarnation" is "gilgul," like the word "galgal," which means "wheel." Just as a point on a wheel after going full circle returns to its original location, likewise does a soul in a body go from birth to death and to birth again through reincarnation.

It is not merely about the recycling of souls. Reincarnation is only meaningful if it allows a person to accomplish in his next life what he failed to achieve in his previous one. It is only purposeful if it helps a person to advance his personal tikun.

This is what life is about: tikun. It is about achieving personal perfection as defined by the Torah:

God said, "Let us make man in Our image, after Our likeness . . ." (Bereishis 1:26)

This was the mandate for the creation of the first man, Adam HaRishon. He was created so perfect that even angels confused him for God.[1] When he sinned by eating from the Aitz HaDa'as Tov v'Ra, the Tree of Knowledge of Good and Evil his reality dramatically changed, impacting not only himself but all of mankind:

> All souls were, in the beginning, part of Adam HaRishon. When he sinned his limbs fell off and his height was reduced. We explained this matter to mean that the souls descended to the depths of the Klipos, and only a few of them remained within him. (Sha'ar HaGilgulim, Introduction 12)

When Adam HaRishon was first created his soul included all the souls of mankind that would come into the world until the Messianic Era.[2] Just as his physical body was made up of countless parts, likewise was his soul comprised of similar parts, on a spiritual level. Each of those parts were souls, as were the smaller components of which they were made.

For example, the spiritual shoulder of Adam HaRishon was comprised of different sections and sub-sections, each of which was either a soul-root

---

[1] Bereishis Rabbah 1:8.
[2] Sha'ar HaGilgulim, Introduction 29.

or an actual soul.[3] This resulted in a hierarchy of souls, since some parts were "higher" in the structure of souls than others. This is detailed extensively in Sha'ar HaGilgulim.

Had Adam HaRishon obeyed God and not eaten from the Aitz HaDa'as Tov v'Ra for three hours[4] until the first Shabbos of Creation, the free will stage of history would have come to a close and the Messianic Era would have begun.[5] There would have been no need for reincarnation.

This of course did not happen. Adam violated the Divine command not to eat, and not only did he not perfect Creation but he reversed much of what had been previously rectified by God.[6] Consequently his spiritual stature was greatly reduced, and the souls which had previously been a part of him, but which were not necessary for his own existence, "fell off" into the Klipos.

What are the Klipos? The word means "peels" because, like a peel, they act as a barrier, in this case between a person and God. There are basically two realities in Creation, pure and impure, and the Klipos are the basis of the latter.

The origin of the Klipos is a major discussion in Kabbalah.[7] The main point is that they exist to

---

[3] The right shoulder corresponded to Hevel and the left shoulder to Kayin (Sha'ar HaGilgulim, Introduction 35).

[4] Three hours on the level on which Adam HaRishon had first been created was equal to hundreds of years on our level of spiritual existence (Drushei Olam HaTohu, Chelek 2, Drush 3, Anaf 22).

[5] Drushei Olam HaTohu, Drush Aitz HaDa'as, Siman 12.

[6] Drushei Olam HaTohu, Chelek 1, Ma'amar HaKlalli, Os 4.

[7] Aitz Chaim, Sha'ar 48, Sha'ar HaKlipos.

make evil possible in order for man to have free will, the main purpose of Creation.[8] As the Midrash explains, when God said "very good" regarding the sixth day of Creation He referred to the creation of the yetzer hara, the evil inclination and representative of the Klipos "within" man.[9]

The Klipos, being completely spiritual, cannot be seen with physical eyes. They can be observed however through the moral chaos they create, and any place which promotes immoral behavior is either impacted or controlled by the Klipos.

All souls that fell into the Klipos must undergo a process of removal from there before they can enter a body and begin their tikun. The process by which a soul leaves the Klipos, enters a body, carries out rectification and achieves perfection, includes reincarnation. This is because it is ongoing and often requires several lifetimes to complete.

Leaving the Klipos is not a simple process, and the greater the soul the more difficult it is:

> Whenever a soul is very great it is not possible to remove it from the Klipos except through trickery and scheming[10] . . . (Sha'ar HaGilgulim, Introduction 38).

---

[8] Drushei Olam HaTohu, Chelek 2, Drush 5, Anaf 2, Siman 5.
[9] Bereishis Rabbah 9:9. Every person has a specific klipah that remains attached to him or her through their lives (Sha'ar HaGilgulim, Introduction 23).
[10] Hebrew: mirmah u'tachboles. This will be discussed in a later chapter.

It can be easier for a soul to leave the Klipos than for the Klipos to leave a soul. Just as a person can be negatively influenced by his environment even after leaving it, likewise a soul remains impacted by the Klipos after leaving them. Rabbi Chaim Vital wrote this regarding his own extraction from the Klipos:

> Since this is the first time I am leaving the depth of the Klipos, it has been a big struggle [for me] to overcome my [evil] inclination. This is the reason for my constant sadness and self-concern. (Sha'ar HaGilgulim, Introduction 38)

Once a soul has left the Klipos and entered a body it begins the process of rectification on the levels of Nefesh, Ruach, and Neshamah. This occurs primarily through the performance of positive mitzvos and by not transgressing negative commandments, which makes possible complete tikun in a single lifetime.

Possible, but often not likely. Most people spend entire lifetimes rectifying only portions of the levels, necessitating reincarnation to complete incomplete stages of the tikun process. A person will continue to reincarnate until he has achieved rectification, or history runs out of time.[11]

It would be pointless if every time a person

---

[11] As the Talmud states there is a final time for the arrival of Moshiach (Sanhedrin 98a).

reincarnated he began his tikun all over again. Whatever prevented him from rectification the first time could do so in subsequent gilgulim as well. After many lifetimes a person could be no further ahead with respect to his personal tikun than he was when he first began.

To avoid this problem, whatever is rectified in a previous lifetime is not subject to negative change in a future one. Instead the completed portion of a level of soul is set aside for future benefit, like money locked away in a trust fund.[12] It can return in a future gilgul to help a person rectify other parts of his soul, but the rectified portion will not be damaged if the person sins.[13]

For example, if a person rectified only 50 percent of his Nefesh in his first lifetime he will reincarnate to rectify the remaining 50 percent. The rectified half may or may not return with the unrectified half, but if does it will not be impacted by any sins committed in the second body. It will benefit from the mitzvos performed but not be held accountable for the transgressions that occur.

If after reincarnating the person rectifies only an additional 25 percent of his Nefesh he will reincarnate to rectify the balance. Even if the rectified 75 percent returns as well it will only benefit from the mitzvos but not be affected by the sins. The same thing is true for the levels of Ruach and

---

[12] Sha'ar HaGilgulim, Introduction 14.
[13] Sha'ar HaGilgulim, Introduction 3.

Neshamah as well.

If a person manages to rectify his entire Nefesh, Ruach, and Neshamah, he will no longer need to reincarnate and his soul can remain in Heaven.[14] If he does not complete any of the three levels in his first lifetime, then even after completing the tikun of one level the rule is that he will have to die and reincarnate in order to begin rectification of the next level.[15]

An example would be someone who during his first life dies before completing the tikun of his Nefesh. Even though in his reincarnation he completes his Nefesh, he cannot receive his Ruach to rectify until he dies and reincarnates again.[16] This is true even if he is still young at the time.

This explains on a Kabbalistic level why some people die "early."[17] If they did not, young and unable to receive their next level of soul to rectify, the person would spiritually stagnate, perhaps even reverse some of the tikun they did achieve during that lifetime. They would certainly lose valuable time better spent on rectifying their next level of soul.

For some the rectification process is not so straightforward. Past sins can be so severe that a person cannot yet reincarnate as a human. Instead, her or she may reincarnate as an animal,

---

[14] He can, however, return for the benefit of others, an idea that will be discussed in a future session.

[15] Sha'ar HaGilgulim, Introduction 2.

[16] There are exceptions, but they are not the norm.

[17] Sha'ar HaGilgulim, Introduction 35.

vegetation, or something inanimate like a rock:

> Bilaam the Evil,[18] who was a snake charmer,
> only had power in his mouth and was able to
> curse people effectively. Therefore, when Bi-
> laam was killed he reincarnated into a specif-
> ic rock, the level of the inanimate,[19] to atone
> for the snake charming he did with his
> mouth. (Sha'ar HaGilgulim, Introduction 22)

The Talmud explains that Divine judgment is
always measure-for-measure, which means that
for the sake of tikun "the punishment always fits
the crime."[20] This is true of reincarnation as well,
which means that a person's reincarnation will be
based upon the sin he or she committed in a previous lifetime.

This, of course, is not clear to anyone living in
the current period time. People only see tragedy,
suffering, and what seems like Divine injustice as
some people struggle with either physical or spiritual handicaps. It is clear, however, from Sha'ar
HaGilgulim that Divine justice incorporates more
than just the present. It specifically takes into account the past and the future as well.[21]

---

[18] The sorcerer hired to curse the Jewish people at the end of the
40 years in the desert (Bamidbar 22:4)
[19] "Domaim" in Hebrew, which means "silent."
[20] Sanhedrin 90a.
[21] Sha'ar HaGilgulim, Introduction 22.

six reasons to reincarnate

THOUGH EVERYONE TODAY is a reincarnation, not everyone throughout history has reincarnated. Reincarnation is not like other aspects of life which are universal and automatic. A soul has to have a reason to reincarnate.

> Souls reincarnate for several reasons, the first being that a person transgressed one of the laws of the Torah and returns to rectify it. (Sha'ar HaGilgulim, Introduction 8)

There are 613 mitzvos in the Torah, 365 of which are negative commandments, "activities" which are forbidden by the Torah. Should a person perform such forbidden acts he has an immediate obligation to do teshuvah and achieve atonement.

This includes not committing the same sin when the opportunity to do so again arises in the future.

Should a person die before rectifying his sin he will have to reincarnate to do so. However, the Arizal explains, since he is reincarnating to rectify a negative mitzvah he will remain prone to sin in his future reincarnation as well.

> The second [reason to reincarnate] is to rectify a mitzvah that it is missing. (Sha'ar HaGilgulim, Introduction 8)

There 248 positive mitzvos in the Torah, each involving an act that must be performed at certain times. If a person dies before having performed all positive mitzvos relevant to him he will have to reincarnate to complete what he is missing. Since, however, it is a positive mitzvah that has caused the person to reincarnate, he will not be prone to sin in a future reincarnation.[1]

Not every positive mitzvah applies to every Jew, however. Some positive mitzvos apply only to kohanim or levi'im. Other mitzvos are circumstantial, like divorce and sending away the mother bird,[2] while Bris Milah is a mitzvah that applies

---

[1] Why should he be more prone to sin in a future lifetime if in a previous one he avoided transgressing a negative commandment?

[2] "If you come across a bird's nest on a tree or upon the ground, containing chicks or eggs, and the mother bird is roosting upon the chicks or upon the eggs, then you must not take the mother along with the young. You shall surely send away the mother and only then take the young, in order that it might be good for you and so that you shall merit length of days." (Devarim 22:6-7)

only to a male child.[3]

Some mitzvos cannot be performed in every generation. For example, some are only applicable during Temple times, such as sacrifices, while others, like the establishment of a Sanhedrin, require certain preexisting conditions. Is a person considered to be "lacking" if he or she has yet to fulfill such commandments?

The question is pertinent since tradition teaches that every mitzvah corresponds to a different part of the human body. The 248 positive mitzvos correspond to the 248 limbs of a person, and the 365 negative mitzvos to the 365 tendons. Thus the performance of every mitzvah rectifies a different part of a person's body, implying that all mitzvos do apply to every Jew at least on some level. How does that work?[4]

> The third [reason to reincarnate] is that [the soul] comes for others, to guide and rectify them. (Sha'ar HaGilgulim, Introduction 8)

In this third scenario the soul does not need to reincarnate for its own benefit. This means that it has fulfilled all necessary positive mitzvos and has rectified all past transgressions. Technically-speaking it no longer requires any form of reincarnation.

---

[3] If by the age of 13 a boy has not yet been circumcised the mitzvah becomes his to fulfill.
[4] This will be answered in a future session.

This does not mean though that it cannot or won't return in a future reincarnation for the benefit of others. It can and often reincarnates in the body of another person as an "additional soul," to help the "host" to grow spiritually in ways that he desires but of which he may be incapable on his own, something called in Sha'ar HaGilgulim called "ibur," or "impregnation.

> In the first [situation the reincarnated soul] can easily sin since it originally sinned [in its previous life]. In the second [case], it is unlikely to sin, but in the third [scenario], it certainly will not sin. (Sha'ar HaGilgulim, Introduction 8)

As mentioned previously, reincarnation is in order to rectify what was left spiritually incomplete or blemished. It is not in order to start again and perhaps get wrong the next time what was accomplished the previous times. Consequently, the spiritual level on which a person leaves one life greatly impacts the level on which he will return in future reincarnations.

> There are other reasons [for reincarnation], which are: Sometimes he will reincarnate to marry his soul mate because he did not merit to marry her the first time. (Sha'ar HaGilgulim, Introduction 8)

This is a topic of interest unto itself. The concept of a "soul mate," of a "match made in Heaven," resonates with peoples all over the world. Just as there is potential for physical "chemistry" between people, including between siblings and friends as well, there is also potential for spiritual chemistry.

There is a big difference between the two, however. Physical chemistry is superficial and can end as fast as it begins. Soul chemistry is eternal. Physical chemistry can interfere with spiritual growth, but soul chemistry enhances the physical aspect of a relationship while it strengthens its spiritual component.

This is why it requires merit to meet one's soul mate. Unworthy people can easily meet and enter a relationship with a physically attractive person. It is spiritual merit, however, that brings together people who are destined to be united on the level of their souls, because it is not something that happens by chance. It is something that happens because Heaven makes it possible:

> Know that when a man is "new," that is, it is his first time in the world, then his soul mate is born with him, as it is known. When it comes time to marry her "they" make it possible for him [to do so] quickly, and free of any trouble whatsoever. (Sha'ar HaGilgulim, Introduction 20)

The journey to one's first reincarnation is a long one, but once a soul finally is in a body of its own it begins its history with a relatively clean slate. There is much work to do to achieve tikun, and life will be filled with tests and many spiritual opportunities. However, being fresh out of the Klipos and "new" at it, there is Divine dispensation and assistance,[5] including the opportunity to readily meet one's soul mate.

This is not the case should a person die needing to reincarnate to rectify what was left over at the end of his previous life:

> If this man committed a sin and needs to reincarnate . . . and his soul mate will also reincarnate for his benefit, when it comes time to marry her, they will not make it possible for him [to do so] quickly, but after much trouble. Since he returned because of some sin there are [Heavenly] "accusers" who want to keep her from him, causing them to fight. With respect to this it says, "It is as difficult to pair them as the splitting of the Red Sea." (Sha'ar HaGilgulim, Introduction 20)

It is explained that a person can marry a non-soul mate and still have a "good" marriage. He may not meet his exact match, but he can marry someone who comes from the same spiritual "vicinity" of his soul making spiritual compatibility possible. There have been many viable mar-

---

[5] Sha'ar HaGilgulim, Introduction 38.

riages throughout history that have not brought together actual soul mates, and will not until the Messianic Era.[6]

If a person has such a marriage after he has already married his soul mate in a previous reincarnation, then he will not have to reincarnate to marry her. If he has yet to marry his soul mate then this itself becomes a reason to reincarnate as many times as necessary until Heaven deems fit to make the match.

All of this has been talking about a standard reincarnation. This is when a person dies and his soul returns in another body to complete its tikun. Just as the body belonged to the soul in the previous lifetime it belongs to the soul in the current one as well. Each body cannot survive without its soul.

There is, however, another form of reincarnation in which the soul does not go into a body of its own. Rather it enters the body that belongs to another soul, and it can do this while the person is already alive and leave it without killing the person. As mentioned previously, this form of reincarnation is called, "Ibur," or "Impregnation."[7]

There are basically two reasons for ibur. The first reason is for the benefit of the guest soul. The ibur itself does not require additional tikun, but has come down into the person's body to help and guide him to accomplish spiritual objectives be-

---

[6] Sha'ar HaGilgulim, Introduction 8
[7] Sha'ar HaGilgulim, Introduction 5.

yond the host's soul capacity to achieve.

Perhaps the most famous ibur is that of Pinchas ben Elazar ben Aharon HaKohen. The Arizal revealed:

> The soul comes to a person when he is born b'sod an actual reincarnation . . . A soul that comes b'sod ibur after a person is born, for example the Nefesh of Nadav and Avihu that became an ibur in Pinchas . . . (Sha'ar HaGilgulim, Introduction 32)

Pinchas was the zealot who killed Zimri, the prince of the tribe of Shimon, during the fiasco with the women of Midian.[8] Until that point in time he was a virtual nobody, not even a kohen since he was born prior to the giving of the Torah. As the Midrash says he was a zealot in waiting.[9]

For ending the Chillul Hashem—profanation of God's Name—and stopping the plague, Pinchas received several rewards. The first was that Pinchas received Divine attention and credit for saving the Jewish people:

> God spoke to Moshe, saying "Pinchas the son of Elazar the son of Aharon the kohen has turned My anger away from the Children of Israel by his zealously avenging Me among them, so that I did not destroy the Children of

---

[8] Bamidbar 25:1.
[9] Bamidbar Rabbah 20:24.

Israel because of My zeal." (Bamidbar 25:10-11)

The second reward was that he finally became a kohen:

"I therefore give him My covenant of peace. It shall be for him and for his descendants after him [as] an eternal covenant of kehunah, because he was zealous for his God and atoned for the Children of Israel." (Bamidbar 25:12-13)

And not just any kohen, but the Kohen Moshiach, the one who led the Jewish people into battle. His greatest reward though, was the one that the Torah does not mention, perhaps because it is mystical, involving the matter of reincarnation. The Ba'al HaTurim however, says it straight out: Pinchas is Eliyahu.[10]

How did that happen? It is a somewhat long and Kabbalistic story. It began with an act of zealousness thousands of years ago, but it still has yet to end. Eliyahu HaNavi will be the one to herald the arrival of Moshiach and the Final Redemption.

The Arizal further elaborates:

[When] a soul comes b'sod ibur after a person is born . . . it is necessary for another new soul spark to come with it, that is, one for

---

[10] Ba'al HaTurim, Bamidbar 25:12.

which it is the first time coming into the world, and which is not old and reincarnated. This new soul joined the Nefesh of Nadav and Avihu [with the soul of Pinchas], coming b'-sod ibur with the Nefesh of Pinchas, which was an actual reincarnation. (Sha'ar HaG-ilgulim, Introduction 32)

When a soul is "born" into a body they become inseparable, except through death. When a soul enters a body b'sod ibur, the body has already been alive for some time, and it will remain alive even if the ibur later leaves. The connection between the ibur-soul and the body is less strong than that of the original soul giving life to the body. In the case of Pinchas, the ibur were the souls of Nadav and Avihu.[11]

Nadav and Avihu do not have much of a history in the Torah, but they do in history in general. From the Torah they seem like "bad guys,"[12] but in Kabbalah they are rather heroic. Their lives and deaths do not consume many verses in the Torah, but their souls after leaving this world had great impact on many important people in Tanach, aside from Pinchas.

----

[11] Even though these were two souls, the Zohar (Acharei 57b) explains that they count as "two halves of a single" soul because of their unique and inherent connection to one another.

[12] They died by a fire that came out from the Holy of Holies when they brought an "unauthorized fire" for the altar (Vayikra 10:1). There is much discussion as to exactly what the sin was that caused their deaths, since they made a few tragic mistakes, like gazing at the Divine Presence on top of Mt. Sinai at the time of the giving of Torah (Rashi, Shemos 24:10).

As a result of this weaker connection, apparently, the ibur has difficulty remaining attached to the host body on its own. It requires an additional soul, specifically a "new" soul that has yet to reincarnate into a body, to join and increase its "adhesion" to the host soul. The souls of Nadav and Avihu may have qualified Pinchas to become a kohen,[13] but it was the new soul that changed his personna altogether:

> It was necessary for another [new soul] to be an ibur in Pinchas, another new Nefesh, and it was called by the name "Eliyahu HaTishbi" from the inhabitants of Gilad, from the root of Gad. It was a new soul as mentioned and it came then in order to connect and join together the Nefesh of Nadav and Avihu with the Nefesh of Pinchas himself, which was a complete reincarnation from the day of his birth. (Sha'ar HaGilgulim, Introduction 32)

This is how Pinchas morphed into Eliyahu the Prophet. His original soul remained the host soul of his body. Receiving the Nefesh of both Nadav and Avihu turned him into a prophet.[14] The addition of the soul of Eliyahu HaTishbi turned

---

[13] Usually a kohen who kills another person, even for the right reason, cannot officiate as a kohen. However, apparently Pinchas died momentarily after killing Zimri and before receiving the ibur of Nadav and Avihu, making him like a new creation and therefore, eligible to be a kohen.

[14] Nadav and Avihu make people prophets.

him into Eliyahu the Prophet, but only after the addition of another soul:

> [Pinchas] further required another new soul as well in order to connect and join the new soul called "Eliyahu HaTishbi" with the rest of the old souls, the Nefesh of Pinchas and Nadav and Avihu. Therefore, it was necessary for an additional new soul to come into Pinchas which was also called "Eliyahu," [except that it came] from the root of Binyomin. (Sha'ar HaGilgulim, Introduction 32)

The same way that the souls of Nadav and Avihu required a new soul to help them remain with the soul of Pinchas, likewise that soul required an additional new soul to bond it to the others souls. It was called "Eliyahu HaGiladi," and with it Pinchas became Eliyahu HaNavi, and eventually the angel of the same name who ascended to Heaven on a fiery chariot[15] and will usher in the Final Redemption.

When the ibur is of this nature then the additional souls understandably benefit from the mitzvos performed by their host, but do not share in the responsibility of sins committed or any suffering that may result. They came to increase the spiritual potential of the person and therefore remain invulnerable to any negative impact of the ibur.

---

[15] II Melachim 2:11.

This is not the case when the ibur is for the sake of the guest soul. This happens when the visiting soul has its own tikun to complete, which it will do on the spiritual shoulders of another soul experiencing the same tikun. Though this is to the ibur's advantage there is also risk involved.

An example can be someone who has yet to be involved in the mitzvah of divorce. Throughout each of his previous gilgulim he has managed to stay married and has therefore never undergone the kind of tikun that might result from such a mitzvah. Or perhaps, he has never been a kohen and able to perform the mitzvos unique to kohanim.

He can do this and other mitzvos as well through someone else performing the missing mitzvos. He can, as per the example, come as an ibur in a person who is undergoing a divorce, or in a kohen who is performing a kohen-type mitzvah. When it comes to tikun it only matters that a soul experience it. The body is just a "vehicle" to make the performance of mitzvos possible.

Since however, the ibur has come for its own benefit, though it can incidentally benefit the host body, it will share in its sins, and therefore its suffering, as well. Of course it will not be faulted for a sin but it can, while in the body, be impacted by it.

One of the main properties of an ibur is that it can come and go during the lifetime of the host. It never bonds with the body like the host soul so that its removal will cause death. Its appearance will enhance a person spiritually and its removal can cause the person to spiritually descend, but it won't directly cause his death.

It can however remain in the host body for the rest of its life if the person maintains the level of merit that brought it in the first place. Should that be the case there is an additional and remarkable benefit for the host soul that goes beyond its life in this world, into Olam HaBa, or the World-to-Come.

The Talmud explains that this world is not the one in which we are rewarded for the mitzvos we performed.[16] Our bodies, as they presently exist, could never survive the reward of even a "simple" mitzvah, let alone the more complicated and complex ones. We have to first transform to a far more etherial state with a greatly enhanced spiritual capacity before that can happen.

The final level of each person, at least in the early stages of the World-to-Come, will not be the same as another.[17] Some souls by virtue of their inherent spiritual level are destined for higher planes of the World-to-Come than souls that originated on a lower spiritual level.[18] The only mitigating factor will be the mitzvos or sins performed while in this world.

In a world in which there is no yetzer hara and there is perfect spiritual clarity, there will be no jealousy. Even as early as Yemos HaMoshiach

---

[16] Kiddushin 39b.
[17] Yevamos 47a.
[18] Bava Basra 75a.

jealousy of others will be a thing of the past. Without the yetzer hara to delude us,[19] we will only blame ourselves for what we could have achieved but did not.

There is another way to impact one's level in the World-to-Come. Ibur. Should a person merit to keep his ibur until he leaves this world, and the guest soul is destined for a higher level in the World-to-Come than the host soul, the former can elevate the latter to its level. A soul can actually go beyond its eternal level on the "back" of another more elevated soul.

As a person strives to increase his level of spirituality and come closer to God, he may only "see" some of the more immediate benefits of doing so. If his will to improve however, goes beyond his personal capacity to do so, he will "inspire" Heaven to boost his ability with the addition of a soul, an ibur.

Once this occurs, and he maintains the ibur for the rest of his life, he will experience more than additional success in this world. He will later find himself on a level in the World-to-Come he could never have hoped to achieve with his personal soul own alone.

---

[19] Succah 52a.

seven
leaving the klipos

AS MENTIONED PREVIOUSLY, all souls were originally part of the soul of Adam HaRishon until he sinned. Once that happened, any soul that was not necessary for him to survive "fell off" and into the depths of the Klipos. This is where they remain until they are elevated from the Klipos and begin their journey to tikun through reincarnation.

It is not a straight path to incarnation. Perhaps the best way to explain this is to use Rabbi Chaim Vital's personal example.

To begin with, just as the world of holiness is not uniform, containing levels, so does the world of Klipos lack uniformity, having its own levels as well. The deeper a soul fell into the Klipos the greater the impact they will have on it, and the more difficulty the soul will have leaving them.

What determined the depth in the Klipos to which a soul fell? The general rule is, the holier the soul, the deeper it fell into the Klipos.[1] Spiritually weak souls did not fall deep into the Klipos and can leave them relatively easily. Greater souls, however, fell deeper into the Klipos and have a more difficult time leaving them.

Though you can take the soul from the Klipos you cannot completely take the klipah from the soul:

> There is not one soul that does not have one level of klipah, made for it like personal clothing, based upon the level of its sin while it was included in Adam HaRishon when he sinned, as mentioned. This klipah clothes it, encasing it all around its entire life. Thus the soul which is holy and spiritual is clothed within the impure klipah. (Sha'ar HaGilgulim, Introduction 23)

Since every person has his own personal klipah, he has his own personal yetzer hara as well. This is what the Talmud implies when it says:

> The greater the person, the greater the evil inclination. (Succah 52a).

This is why, Rabbi Vital explains, great peo-

---

[1] Sha'ar HaGilgulim, Introduction 27.

ple make mistakes that lesser people might not. The spiritually weaker person may not be drawn towards the sin whereas the greater soul might have difficulty resisting it. Culpability though is something only God can decide, and every person must try their best to avoid any kind of sin.

What determines the time of departure of a soul from the Klipos, and how does it leave them?

It is God Who determines the departure time of a soul from the Klipos. As the rabbis have taught:

> Do not be disrespectful of any person and do not be dismissing of any thing. There is no person who does not have his hour, and there is no thing which does not have its place. (Pirkei Avos 4:3)

It is the master plan for Creation that determines the needs of history at any given moment in time, and the souls necessary to fulfill those needs. When history requires a particular soul to come into the world then Divine Providence arranges events so that they result in a soul's departure from the Klipos.

This is the deeper reason for the following:

> Rebi Yitzchak asked, "Why were our ancestors barren? Because The Holy One, Blessed is He, desires the prayers of the righteous." (Yevamos 64a)

This is about more than just staying in touch with God:

> Through our prayers and intentions, the sparks of the seven "kings" that died,[2] which are the 288 Sparks,[3] are separated [from the Klipos] and elevated [from them] . . . Every prayer, according to the intention with which it is said and the merit of the time at which it is said, separates a fixed amount of the 288 Sparks. (Aitz Chaim, Sha'ar 39, Drush 2)

Though this is talking about sparks and not souls it means the same thing, because a soul is just a particular type of holy spark. And, just as prayer separates and elevates a soul from the Klipos, so do activities such a the performance of mitzvos, the using of materials, and even eating.[4]

Everything contains holy sparks. They are spiritual light, but they are also potential, like spiritual fuel locked away in every aspect of Creation. Prayer requires energy, and holy sparks provide it. The same is true of mitzvos, and sins for that matter, and doing either "consumes" holy sparks.

The difference is what happens after the sparks have been consumed. When a spark is used

---

[2] These are the pre-Creation sefiros that broke to prepare the way for Creation, and whose names are taken from the end of Parashas Vayishlach (Bereishis 36:31-39).

[3] These are the sparks that fell into the Klipos after Sheviras HaKeilim in order to maintain the "broken pieces" from which Creation would be made (Da'as Elokim).

[4] Sha'ar HaGilgulim, Introduction 38.

in a holy manner it is ready to ascend as it is. When it used for a sin it must first be purified before it can ascend, which means that the person must be punished or when possible, repent before he is.

When something from Creation is processed, holy sparks are used up. The holier the usage the more sparks are consumed and elevated. Eating separates out and elevates sparks. Eating with specific intention to elevate sparks separates out more sparks and elevates them even higher. Making a blessing before eating enhances the entire process and increases the tikun power of the act.

One of the most powerful ways to elevate souls out of the Klipos is through the death of righteous people. This is particularly true when evil is rampant, as was the case at the time the Ten Martyrs went to their deaths at the hands of the Romans. They died sanctifying the Divine Name, and the greater the sanctification the more sparks were elevated and Creation was rectified.[5]

In truth, it is really a battle of tug-of-war. As much as history requires holy sparks to be extricated from the Klipos, the Klipos want to maintain their hold on holy sparks. Firstly, the Klipos survive because of the holiness they draw from the sparks among them, and secondly, they know that important souls play important roles in the redemption process, and therefore, their demise.[6]

---

[5] Aitz Chaim, Sha'ar HaKlallim, Ch. 1.
[6] Sha'ar HaGilgulim, Introduction 20.

The greater the soul the more this is true.

The spiritual battle means that a certain amount of subterfuge, called "mirmah u'tachboles," or "trickery and scheming," must be employed, as Rabbi Vital explains with respect to himself:

> Know that whenever a soul is very great, it is not possible to remove it from the Klipos except through trickery and scheming, like what happened to me. The Chitzonim had thought that I was already lost among them, God forbid, and did not become suspicious when The Holy One, Blessed is He, took me from among them to be a Tzelem-Encompassing [Light] over HaRav "Maggid Mishneh." They thought just the opposite, that it would be to their benefit,[7] but I ended up becoming their enemy [by strengthening the HaRav Maggid Mishneh instead]. (Sha'ar HaGilgulim, Introduction 38)

The "Maggid Mishneh" is a commentary on the "Yad Chazakah" of the Rambam. His actual name was Rav Vidal of Tolosa, and he lived during the second half of the fourteenth century. He was also the first "location" of the soul spark of Rabbi Chaim Vital after he left the Klipos. This is the reason for the similar names, "Vidal" and "Vital."

---

[7] They thought that he would cause the Maggid Mishneh to further sin.

When a person leaves the Klipos it is not immediately into a body, as the following explains:

> Know that for all the souls in the depths of the Klipos it is impossible for them to be taken out from there and to immediately reincarnate. They have to [first] come three times b'sod Tzelem, as an "Encompassing Light" over three people from the same root. After that, [the departing soul spark] will be able to reincarnate and come to the world b'sod an actual Inner [Light]. This is considered to be the first reincarnation. (Sha'ar HaGilgulim, Introduction 38)

When the time comes for a spark to the leave the Klipos it first joins another person, already living, whose soul also comes from the same soul root. Unlike an ibur though, it does not enter the person and join the host soul. Rather, it remains a spark and "hovers" over the host person like an encompassing light. This is called a "Tzelem."

When the host person dies, the spark then goes and becomes a Tzelem over a second person, also from the same root as the Tzelem. When this person dies the spark becomes a Tzelem over a third person from its root, completing this phase of the reincarnation process once the third host dies. The spark is ready to reincarnate into a body of its own. Thus, what we may view as the first reincarnation of a soul is really its fourth time around, though its first time in its own body.

It is the klipah with which a person leaves the realm of impurity that creates his or her personal spiritual challenge. It is this which pulls a person in a direction that is contrary to the will of God, to give a person the opportunity to persevere and to will to overcome this negative leaning. This is what eventually results in spiritual growth now, and eternal reward in Olam HaBa.

One of the defining factors of a righteous person is that he knows this about life and commits himself to the struggle:

> The Highest Wisdom decreed that man should consist of two opposites. These are his pure spiritual soul and his unenlightened physical body. Each one is drawn toward its nature, so that the body inclines toward the material, while the soul leans toward the spiritual. The two are then in a constant state of battle. (Derech Hashem 1:2:1-1:3:2)

This is what the tzaddik does his or her entire life: struggle with their klipah. They learn Torah to find out what they need to do and then pay attention to what they have difficulty doing. Mitzvos tend to go against "human nature," or rather, a person's klipah, and therefore, help to reveal a person's yetzer hara and one's personal spiritual battle in life.

It is a radically different approach to life. Most people use their strengths to accomplish goals and either accept their weaknesses or work around them. The average person does not see life as the opportunity to use personal strengths to overcome personal weakness.

There are obvious consequences of such an approach to life, and some not so obvious consequences. The obvious one is that a person will not fulfill his potential to overcome his human nature in order to develop his Divine nature. He will live spiritually unfulfilled and leave spiritually incomplete, necessitating suffering and reincarnation.

The less obvious consequence of a non-Torah approach to life is something Kabbalah calls, "Chavut HaKever," literally the "Beating in the Grave," detailed here:

> After a person dies and is buried in the ground, immediately four angels come and lower the ground of the grave. They deepen it below resulting in an hollow the height of the person buried there . . . Then they return his soul to his body like during his life, the reason being that klipah is still attached to the soul and the body and has not separated from them. Therefore the soul must be returned to the body as one. Then each of the angels mentioned holds an end, and they shake him and beat him with sticks of fire, similar to the way a garment is held from its two ends and shaken to remove dust that is stuck to it, until the klipah separates from him completely. Therefore, this is called the "Beating in the Grave," which is similar to [the way] a person

beats and shakes his garment. Thus, they need to deepen the grave so that there will be space in which to shake and beat him. (Sha'ar HaGilgulim, Introduction 23)

The reason for this post-mortem treatment is mentioned as well:

It is already known from what they, z"l, say in Pirkei Rebi Eliezer how an angel comes to a person in his grave and asks him, "What is your name?" The person answers, "It is revealed and known before Him, may He be blessed, that I do not know my name, etc." (Sha'ar HaGilgulim, Introduction 23)

It may be astounding that this is the one question that they ask a person after death, and even more astounding that he cannot answer it. The following explains the meaning of all of this:

Every person has two names, one from the side of holiness [given by his parents at birth], and one from the side of klipah. If the person, while living in this world, is able to ascertain and know the name of the klipah within him, he can then investigate from where it came, and which level it is on . . . This way he can know the place of the blemish and the kind of rectification he requires. He can easily rectify the blemish and in this way the klipah can be easily separated from him during his life. He will not need to separate it from him through the beating in the grave at all. Therefore, when a righteous person dies they don't ask him the name from the Sitra Achra, because during his lifetime he troubled himself and endured suffering to separate the klipah from him, as mentioned, so it is easy to complete the separation through the beating in the grave. (Sha'ar HaGilgulim, Introduction 23)

Do angels actually visit the grave of a person after death and physically deepen it for those in need of chavut hakever? It doesn't matter if this is true physically or only spiritually, because either way the consequence is real and experienced by the soul. The righteous person knows this and spends his life doing what he must to avoid the after death experience.

For an evil person however, it is just the opposite: he caused [his klipah] to become strongly attached, requiring great beatings and punishments to separate it from him through the beating in the grave. Had he known during his lifetime the name from the Sitra Achra he could have rectified, during his lifetime, the name from the Sitra Achra. Hence, they give them intense beatings because they did not know their names as mentioned. They did not investigate to know it in their lifetimes because they did not want to make the effort to act in the way that right-eous people trouble themselves. (Sha'ar HaGilgulim, Introduction 23)

When a person overcomes his yetzer hara to sin he has done more than mitzvah. He has, in fact, weakened the attachment of his personal klipah to him, making him less susceptible to its machinations. He becomes less prone to confuse the voice of the yetzer hara for his own and will not readily do its bidding, if at all.

They tell a story about the Chofetz Chaim[8] that illustrates this point:

The Chofetz Chaim died at the age of 94. One day in his old age he awoke and was confronted by his yetzer hara. "Old man," it began to tempt, "why do you arise so early in the morning? Surely after such a long life of devotion to the service of God you deserve to sleep a little later!"

Unfazed by the wiles of his yetzer hara, the Chofetz Chaim answered him back, "If YOU are up this early in the morning then there is no reason why I should not be up as well!"

Did this conversation actually take place between the great and venerable sage and his yetzer

---

[8] Rabbi Yisroel Meir HaKohen Kagan, born in Zhetel, Poland on January 26, 1839, and died in Radun, Wilno Voivodship in Poland (now Belarus) on September 15, 1933.

hara? Probably not in so many words. Rather, he acted as if he had, meaning that he felt like waking up later, "heard" the justification to do so after so many years of rising in the morning on time, but chose to ignore it knowing that it was only yetzer hara, and not him, who actually thought that way. He knew the name of his klipah well.

The Chofetz Chaim, and other great people like him, worked on leaving the Klipos their entire lives. They did not do it only once after being a Tzelem three times over others and entering a body of their own. They continuously did it so that by the time they died, if they hadn't left the Klipos completely, they had done so enough to warrant at least only a minor "beating in the grave."

Not many people work on themselves spiritually to such an extent. Most people have no idea what the Klipos are, let alone what to do about them. They are so concerned about physical survival and material gain that they have little interest or time to work on spiritual completion.

This is why the Klipos seem so much in charge of history. They are. Through the billions of people to which they are attached, and who have no knowledge of their existence or their mandate, they can impose their will on mankind. All the hatred, killing, promiscuity, and flagrant abuse of life stems from the klipah attached to each individual who does not endeavor to loosen its control over his or her life.

Spiritually desensitized, such people are able to act selfishly as if it is their natural born right.

Their klipah, as the name implies, acts as a barrier between their consciousness and inner sense of Godliness, opening the door for them to pursue more base instincts. In some people the klipah is so strong that it reduces them to little more than an animal.

The journey of life is the journey away from the Klipos. Meaning in life is derived from doing that which weakens their hold over one's consciousness. To ignore the Klipos and let them have their way is to become a slave to their will. To acknowledge them and work on overcoming them is to increase personal freedom, and to come closer to becoming an Adam Shalaim—a complete person.

eight
famous gilgulim

ANYONE WHO LEARNS Torah is familiar with Moshe Rabbeinu's father-in-law, Yisro. They know that after Moshe was forced to flee Egypt because he killed an Egyptian taskmaster who was beating a Jew,[1] he eventually made his way to Midian. That is where he met Tzipporah his wife and became the son-in-law of Yisro.[2]

They also know that Yisro eventually converted to Judaism after testing every form of idol worship known to man at that time.[3] After hearing about all that God had done for the Jewish people in Egypt to free them, the miracle of the

---

[1] Shemos 2:11-12.
[2] Shemos 2:21.
[3] Shemos Rabbah 1:38.

splitting of the sea, and then about the victory over Amalek, Yisro abandoned all of that and officially became part of the Jewish people.[4] He then returned back to his native Midian to convert the rest of his family,[5] never to be heard from again, at least in the Torah.

It turns out that Yisro had a history, one even before he was born as Yisro:

> In the verse, "If Kayin will be avenged sevenfold" (Bereishis 4:24), [the letters of the Hebrew word for "avenged,"] Yud-Kuf-Mem are the initials of [the names], "Yisro," "Kayin," "Korach," and "Mitzri." (Sha'ar HaGilgulim, Introduction 36)

Even though the word for "avenge," "yukam," has only one Kuf, it is used twice to allude to both Kayin and Korach. The Yud alludes to Yisro, and the Mem to the Mitzri, the Egyptian taskmaster Moshe Rabbeinu killed before fleeing to Midian.

> Since the Nefesh of Kayin is one to which the impurity of the snake latches on a lot, and the evil within it overcomes the good in it, he reincarnated into an Egyptian, who was gentile. (Sha'ar HaGilgulim, Introduction 36)

---

[4] Rashi, Shemos 19:1.
[5] Rashi, Bamidbar 10:30; Mechilta D'Rebi Yishmael, Yisro Amalek 2.

Since the root of Kayin's soul is Gevurah, which constricts the light of God, it is more susceptible to the Klipos and sin. Therefore, Kayin's Klipos-tainted Nefesh eventually reincarnated into the Egyptian taskmaster.

> Moshe, who was Hevel, wanted to rectify him by killing him with the "Ineffable Name," the 42-letter Name [of God], to separate out the evil out from within him and bring it to the level of good, to holiness. (Sha'ar HaGilgulim, Introduction 36)

Moshe Rabbeinu was the reincarnation of Hevel, vis-à-vis Shais first. Thus his name, spelled Mem-Shin-Heh, is also an acronym for "Moshe," "Shais," and "Hevel." As such there was already an inherent relationship between Moshe Rabbeinu and the Egyptian he killed, more so than with any other Egyptian at that time.

The Arizal explains that the killing of the Mitzri served two purposes. It saved Dasan from further beatings, and perhaps more importantly, it helped to rectify the Nefesh of his reincarnated brother, Kayin. This was especially so since Moshe killed the Egyptian by pronouncing the 42-letter Name of God which has the power to cause such rectification.

> Then it entered into Yisro who had also been a gentile at that time. As a result, he too converted, on the day that [Moshe] killed the

Egyptian. (Sha'ar HaGilgulim, Introduction 36)

From the Midrash we know that Yisro converted because of all the miracles God performed for the Jewish people until he arrived at the Jewish camp at the base of Mt. Sinai. His transformation seemed, at most, to be intellectual and nothing more. He is even praised for being able to accept truth in a world of incredible falsehood.

Sod adds a whole new dimension to the discussion about the conversion of Yisro. Before he changed his mind about God, his soul was transformed and his spiritual capacity was enhanced. After his future son-in-law dispensed with the evil Egyptian, Kayin's rectified Nefesh joined up with Yisro's own soul, making conversion to Judaism the inevitable result. Thus it says:

> They say in the Book of the Zohar that the beginning of the rectification of Kayin was through Yisro, as has been explained regarding the verse, "I acquired a man from God" (Bereishis 4:1). (Sha'ar HaGilgulim, Introduction 36)

The level of Kayin's Ruach had its own journey to make along its path to rectification.[6] Regarding the next level up, it says:

---

[6] This will be discussed shortly.

The Neshamah of Kayin went into Yisro after he converted because of the strength of the Nefesh of the Egyptian who had been rectified. At that time, the rectification was completed for the sin of Kayin for having killed Hevel and taking his twin [sister]. (Sha'ar HaGilgulim, Introduction 36)

The Midrash explains the reason for Kayin's jealousy of his brother. Apparently Kayin had been born with only one twin sister while Hevel had been born with two twin sisters, which in those days meant two wives.[7] Kayin murdered his brother for the extra twin sister, and this too had a historical impact down the road:

Now [Kayin as Yisro] fed and supported [his brother Hevel as] Moshe, and sustained him and returned his twin sister to him, who was Tzipporah. (Sha'ar HaGilgulim, Introduction 36)

As the Talmud states, even before children are born it is declared in Heaven who will marry whom,[8] which is further explained in Sha'ar HaGilgulim in even more detail.[9] This explanation however takes the concept of zivug to a whole new level, revealing how even marriage can be the

---

[7] Sanhedrin 58b.
[8] Sotah 2a.
[9] Introduction 20; see Session 6.

means to even greater tikun than personal rectification.

Hence, when Yisro extended his hospitality to Moshe, and then later gave his daughter Tzipporah to him as a wife, he was doing more than just extending his family. He was making very right something that had gone very wrong at the beginning of history, as it says:

> This has explained how Kayin did not become rectified from his sin against Hevel except through Yisro, and by way of Moshe, as mentioned. In the beginning it was the killing of the Egyptian [by Moshe Rabbeinu], and in the end it was through Yisro, as mentioned. (Sha'ar HaGilgulim, Introduction 36)

This is just one example of how reincarnation plays a major role in the development of people and the events of history.

❖Korach

The same can be said with respect to Korach, but in a far less complementary manner. The Torah writes:

> Korach the son of Yitzhar, the son of Kehas, the son of Levi took [himself to one side] along with Dasan and Aviram, the sons of Eliav, and On the son of Pelet, descendants of Reuven. They confronted Moshe together with 250 men from the Children of Israel,

chieftains of the congregation, representatives of the assembly, men of repute. They assembled against Moshe and Aharon, and said to them, "You take too much upon yourselves, for the entire congregation are all holy, and God is in their midst. So why do you raise yourselves above God's assembly?" (Bamidbar 15:1-3)

So destructive was Korach's rebellion that what it was and what it did was etched into the collective consciousness of the Jewish people for all time:

So Elazar the kohen took the copper censers which the fire victims had brought, and they hammered them out as an overlay for the altar, as a reminder for the Children of Israel, so that no stranger, who is not of the seed of Aharon, shall approach to burn incense before God, so as not to be like Korach and his congregation . . . (Bamidbar 17:4-5)

Any dispute that is for the sake of Heaven will endure; one that is not for the sake of Heaven will not endure. Which is a dispute that is for the sake of Heaven? The dispute between Hillel and Shammai. Which is a dispute that is not for the sake of Heaven? The dispute of Korach and all his company. (Pirkei Avos 5:17)

Like in all situations when people act in ways that seem unreasonable, the commentators look for explanations as to how Korach could challenge Moshe Rabbeinu and risk so much. What drove Korach to such extreme behavior? This is one level of answer:

> Were they not fools? [Moshe] warned them about it and they [still] took upon themselves to offer [the incense]. They sinned at the cost of their lives, as it says, "the censers of these who sinned at the cost of their lives" (Bamidbar 17:3). What did Korach, who was astute, see [to commit] this folly? His vision deceived him. He saw [prophetically] a chain of great people descended from him, [one of whom was] Shmuel [HaNavi, the great prophet] who is equal [in importance] to Moshe and Aharon. He said, "For his sake I will be spared." [He also saw] 24 watches [of Levi'im] emanating from his grandsons, all prophesying through Ruach HaKodesh . . . He said, "Is it possible that all this greatness is destined to come from me and I should remain silent?" . . . He erred however in thinking that it referred to him. He did not see properly that it was his sons who would repent [and thus did not die at that time]. (Rashi, Bamidbar 16:7)

Even had this been the case though, the risk still may not have justified the action. There had to have been something more fundamentally wrong with Korach to allow him to make such a grave error and drag other important people down with him as well. There was:

> The Ruach [of Kayin] . . . was still mixed together with evil, and that evil entered into Korach, b'sod "And Korach took" (Bamidbar 16:1), that is, he "took" a bad possession to himself. The strength of this evil made him argue with Moshe, who was Hevel his brother, as he had quarreled then [when he was Kayin]. (Sha'ar HaGilgulim, Introduction 36)

When the Nefesh of a person is corrupt, a person can become overly materialistic. The Nefesh, often referred to as the "animal soul," does little to imbue a person spiritually, and is often harnessed by a person to satisfy a drive for material comforts. The Mitzri whom Moshe killed had committed adultery with Dasan's wife, and after catching on, Dasan became the target of the adulterer's blows.[10]

A corrupt Ruach affects a person on a higher level. Korach was after position and prestige, a function of a bloated spirit. He already had a lot of wealth and it did not interest him as much as being a leader of high rank. It made him feel greater than he was.

---

[10] Rashi, Shemos 2:11.

This too was a throwback to Kayin. Kayin's own bloated spirit made him feel that he deserved more than he did, first the extra twin sister and then God's attention after he brought his unworthy sacrifice. He had kept the best for himself, brought second best for God, and expected acceptance as if the reverse was true.

This was also hinted to in Korach's punishment. There were many ways for Moshe Rabbeinu to prove that he was the one whom God supported, but he specifically chose this one:

> "If these men die as all men die and the fate of all men will be occur to them, then God has not sent me. But if God creates a creation, and the earth opens its mouth and swallows them and all that is theirs, and they descend alive into the grave, you will know that these men have provoked God." (Bamidbar 16:29-30)

This form of death might have been considered highly unusual except that the idea has a source in history:

> And God said to Kayin, "Where is Hevel your brother?"
>
> He said, "I do not know. Am I my brother's keeper?"
>
> [God] said, "What have you done? Behold! Your brother's blood cries out to Me from the earth. And now, you are cursed even more

than the ground, which opened its mouth to take your brother's blood from your hand." (Bereishis 4:9-11)

It was thousands of years later, but it was still measure-for-measure. Just as the "mouth" of the earth had swallowed the blood of Hevel, who had become Moshe Rabbeinu, likewise the earth swallowed up Kayin, who had become Korach. It was the closing chapter on a fight that had begun long ago, also over the priesthood.

In fact, when the gematria of "Korach" (308) is subtracted from the gematria of "Moshe" (345), what remains is the gematria of "Hevel" (37).[11] It was s if to say: "Korach, you may make yourself out to be a champion of the people, but you are really Kayin in another body, once again championing your own undeserved cause."

❖Aharon HaKohen

Aharon HaKohen is the symbol of so much that a Jew is supposed to spend his entire life trying to be. He was the brother of the greatest leader mankind will ever know, Moshe Rabbeinu, but his greatness was all his own.

At a crucial moment though he took a tremendous risk that could have cost him his life in this world and in the World-to-Come. In the episode of the golden calf, he was the one who gave the command for all the people to give him their

---

[11] Shem M'Shmuel, Korach 5670.

gold and who put it into the fire as if to make an idol on behalf of the instigators.[12]

He of course had no intention whatsoever to do anything wrong. He saw where the people were going and what had happened to Chur who tried to stop them.[13] Since Har Sinai at that time had the halachic status of the Temple,[14] and Aharon was the Kohen Gadol, murdering him would have meant no atonement for the entire generation.[15] He risked his life to save theirs.

Even though Moshe Rabbeinu later chastised his brother for what he did, even though Aharon acted with the best of intentions, Aharon's act of self-sacrifice seemed nothing less than heroic. He was certainly forgiven by God, because he could never have maintained such a high spiritual role on behalf of the nation if he wasn't.

That is on the level of Pshat. On the level of Sod it is a different story:

> Aharon HaKohen was from the root of Hevel, the son of Adam HaRishon . . . Two soul roots are in the roots of Hevel, and they are the root of Haran, the brother of Avram, and the root of Nachor. Nachor reincarnated into

---

[12] Shemos 32:1.
[13] Shemos Rabbah 16:17.
[14] Ta'anis 16a. The Talmud equates Mount Sinai at the time of the giving of the Torah with the Temple Mount. It returned to the status of a normal mountain on the first of Nissan, when the Mishkan was erected and the Divine Presence moved from the mountain to the golden cover of the Ark (Rashi, Ta'anis 21b).
[15] Sanhedrin 7a.

Chur, the son of Miriam, and Haran reincarnated into Aharon HaKohen. Chur "took" three letters from Nachor . . . Aharon [has the] three letters of Haran, to which an Aleph was added. (Sha'ar HaGilgulim, Introduction 33)

Though it is not always the case, sometimes a person's soul root, at least in Biblical times, was indicated in their actual name. For example, "Nachor" is spelled Nun-Ches-Vav-Raish, the last three letters spelling "Chur." In the case of Aharon, spelled Aleph-Heh-RaishNun, the reverse is true: Haran is part of his name.

Haran came to rectify the sin of Adam HaRishon who worshipped idols. Not only did he not rectify [him], but he furthermore did not believe in God until after Avraham came out of the fiery furnace, as they, z"l, write. Therefore Haran was burned in Ur Kasdim. (Sha'ar HaGilgulim, Introduction 33)

The Midrash explains that Nimrod gave Avraham a choice to reject God, or to burn in a cauldron of fire. Avraham, of course, chose the latter and was prepared to burn to death. Haran, Avraham's brother did not have the same level of belief in God as his brother did, and waited instead to see what would happen to Avraham before choosing sides.

When Avraham miraculously survived the fire, they asked Haran what he believed. Now he confidently responded that he believed in the God of Avraham, and Nimrod's slaves promptly threw him into the fire as well. Miracles, however, do not happen for people who take risks expecting them to occur, and instead Haran burned to death.[16]

Therefore, Haran died and:

> He reincarnated into Aharon to rectify the sin. However, just the opposite occurred when he sinned in the incident of the calf. He should have allowed himself to be killed. It was fitting that he give himself over to be killed when the Mixed Multitude came to him and said, "Arise and make a god for us" (Shemos 32:1). (Sha'ar HaGilgulim, Introduction 33)

From the Torah and the Midrash it seems as if Aharon HaKohen did the heroic thing. It certainly does not seem as if he was expected to give up his life to stop the crowd, something he could have assumed would have happened after seeing Chur die at the hands of the Erev Rav.

This says differently. Not only should Aharon HaKohen have not pretended to fulfill the request of the aggressive Mixed Multitude, even for good reasons, but he was expected to give up his life if only to rectify Haran. Consequently, though he

---

[16] Bereishis Rabbah 38:19.

was forgiven for his sin, Haran still required rectification:

> The sin [of Haran] was not rectified until
> [later in history through] Uriah HaKohen . . .
> (Sha'ar HaGilgulim, Introduction 33)

❖Iyov

One of the most difficult philosophical questions has been: Why do bad things happen to good
people? One of the most difficult examples of this
idea is the story of what happened to Iyov, a nice
guy who had finished "first" until God made a
"bet" with the Satan which dramatically cost Iyov
everything he valued most.

Unlike most people who might consider
themselves righteous and unable to justify the bad
that has happened to them, Iyov was able to ask
God Himself. The answer he received began with:

> Where were you when I founded the earth?
> Tell if you know understanding . . . (Iyov
> 38:4)

What followed was question after question
that eventually made it clear to Iyov that he had
no idea what history was about. When God was
finished, Iyov realized that his evaluation of his
crisis was based upon his small picture view of
history, not God's big picture of history. Iyov was
humbled.

The story itself does not provide much more information than this, though it is enough for an emunah-based life. God knows everything and therefore God knows best. He is not malicious, and wants the best for everyone. We even say that He'd rather see an evil person repent and be saved than suffer punishment and maybe even death. The Talmud sums it this way:

> All that God does He does for the good. (Brochos 60b)

In conclusion, God is never unfair. Sometimes we can see the justice in what He does, often we cannot. On the contrary, sometimes the bad that happens to a person seems so beyond proportion to any evil the person did that it leaves some people thinking that God is not involved in history, or that if He is, He does evil.

Nothing could be further from the truth, especially when gilgulim are part of the equation. When reincarnation is factored in, then negative events can happen in a person's current lifetime based upon sins from previous lifetimes. This is particularly true since the goal of life is tikun, rectification, and that means reincarnating specifically to make amends for past unrectified blemishes.

If Iyov was a perfect example of anything, it was of this, evident by the following:

Terach, Avraham's father, reincarnated into, and was rectified through Iyov. (Sha'ar HaGilgulim, Ch. 36)

Though the Torah only mentions Terach in passing, the Midrash details his life. Not only was he a worshipper of idols, he manufactured them as well.[17] According to the Midrash, he was the one who turned his own son, Avram, into Nimrod when he rejected idol worship and destroyed all the idols in his father's store.[18]

Terach's life began to turn around the day he witnessed his son being miraculously saved from the fire into which Nimrod had him placed in Ur Kasdim. Like many others that day, including Nimrod himself,[19] Terach came to realize that Avraham had been right all along about God.[20] As a result, he left everything behind to journey with his son to Eretz Canaan in order to escape Nimrod, as the Torah says:

Terach took Avram his son, and Lot, the son of Haran, his grandson, and Sarai his daughter-in-law, the wife of Avram his son, and went with them from Ur Kasdim to go to the land of Canaan. (Bereishis 11:31)

---

[17] Bereishis Rabbah 38:19.

[18] Bereishis Rabbah 38:19.

[19] Sefer HaYashar.

[20] The Midrash says that this only occurred after the Angel of Death took the burned body of Haran and threw it down before Terach, proving that Avram had not been saved by magic, but by God (Shochar Tov 118).

When, in Avraham's 70th year, they reached Charan, and Terach saw that Nimrod no longer posed a threat to his family, he settled there instead:

They came as far as Charan and settled there. (Bereishis 11:32)

Five years later, when Avraham was 75 years old, Terach died, never having left Charan:

The days of Terach were 205 years, and Terach died in Charan. (Bereishis 11:32)

It is difficult to imagine that Terach stuck with his idol worshipping ways after leaving Ur Kasdim, especially if he traveled with his son Avraham. Nevertheless, as Rashi points out, he certainly did not die a righteous person and remained in need of tikun.

Apparently he was able to achieve it after reincarnating into Iyov. All that he had gone through as Iyov was what he required to finish off the process of teshuvah he began as Terach. Iyov may not have known this at the time, and his friends who questioned his righteousness certainly did not know it, but it was the entire basis for all that he had gone through.

Even the person reading the story is not informed of this mystical detail. All the reader is privy to is a discussion between God and the Satan regarding the righteousness of Iyov. They "overhear" God handing Iyov over to the Satan to do as he pleases, merely to test Iyov's faith in God, which he does to an extreme.

Many a reader and scholar has left the story of Iyov with several deep and important philosophical questions, usually drawing one of two conclusions. Some decide that the ways of God are too mysterious for man to fathom and that therefore, man must cling to his faith, especially during difficult and confusing times. Others conclude that if there is a God, He does not get overly involved in the affairs of man, if at all. Their viewpoint insists that "injustices" can occur to "good" people.

In the realm of Sod, however, it is a moot point. Beginning with the debate between God and the Satan about the righteous of Iyov, which in and of itself must be understood Kabbalistically, and ending with Iyov's acceptance of his fate, the story is a "lock" in need of a "key." That key, explains Sod, is the soul of Iyov, which was really Terach's reincarnated soul in search of tikun.

Divine justice was served. Divine justice is always served.

nine
moshe rabbeinu

ONE OF THE most famous gilgulim of all time is Moshe Rabbeinu. He is also one of the longest running, coming back in every generation.[1] At the very least, he has to return each generation to rectify the Erev Rav[2] he took out of Egypt against the advice of God.[3] At the very most, he will become Moshiach Ben Dovid and finish the job he began when he first took the Jewish nation out of Egypt.[4]

In truth, Moshe Rabbeinu himself was already a reincarnation of someone else, Shais, who

---

[1] Zohar, Bereishis 25a.
[2] The Mixed Multitude that left Egypt with the Jewish people (Shemos 12:38).
[3] Rashi, Shemos 32:7.
[4] Drushei Olam HaTohu, Drush Aitz HaDa'as 11.

in turn, was the gilgul of Hevel:

> Hevel had a Nefesh and Ruach that were
> damaged; evil was mixed in with good. How-
> ever, his Neshamah was completely good, and
> when they reincarnated to become rectified,
> the Nefesh reincarnated first, as per the or-
> der mentioned, and it was given to Shais, the
> son of Adam HaRishon. The evil that was in it
> left and was given to the evil Bilaam. These
> two levels of the good and evil of the Nefesh
> that were included in Hevel are hinted to in
> his name. The good in it is the [letter] Heh of
> "Hevel," and this was given to Shais as men-
> tioned. (Sha'ar HaGilgulim, Introduction 29)

The story of history is really the story of
Kayin and Hevel, or at least their souls. Hevel did
not live long enough to have offspring, and all of
Kayin's descendants were washed away in the
Flood. Their souls however have lived on and have
been the source of many famous people, good and
bad, throughout history.

Of the two soul sources though, Hevel's seems
to be the principle one, at least in terms of ready-
ing the world for the Final Redemption:

> As a result of the sin of Kayin and Hevel, all
> the souls became mixed together with the
> Klipos, and this is called the mixing of good
> with evil. Since then the souls have been con-
> tinuously separated out from within the Kli-

pos, like the refinement of silver from the waste. This separation will continue until the completion of the separation of the souls . . . Once all the souls will have been separated out completely . . . [the Klipos] will no longer have any life at all and will disappear like smoke, as it says, "Death will be extinct forever" (Yeshayahu 25:8) . . . Thus, the initials of [the Hebrew words for] "Death will be extinct forever" are the letters of "Hevel," to hint that [this will not occur] until all of the reincarnations of Hevel are completed, which are Moshe Rabbeinu reincarnating in every generation to separate out the souls from among the waste. When this has occurred then Moshiach will come and death will be extinct forever. (Sha'ar HaGilgulim, Introduction 20)

Moshe Rabbeinu was born when his mother, Yocheved, was 130 years old. This was not incidental, but alluded to one of his main tasks in history: the rectification of the Erev Rav.

The story of the Erev Rav actually began a long time before the Jewish people were even in Egypt:

Rebi Yirmiyah ben Elazar further stated: In all those years during which Adam was excommunicated he fathered Ruchin, Shiddin, and Lillin, as it says: "And Adam lived 130 years and fathered a son in his own likeness, after his own image" (Bereishis 5:3), from which it follows that until that time he did not father [someone] after his own image. (Eiruvin 18b)

As the Talmud indicates, for 130 years after being expelled from the Garden of Eden, Adam HaRishon did teshuvah. Part of his teshuvah included purging himself of the spiritual impact of the snake, which, apparently, was not without collateral damage:

> All the Shiddin and Ruchin[5] that Adam created during the 130 years that he separated from Chava were holy and elevated souls from the level of Da'as, [except] that [they came into the world] mixed together with the Klipos. This necessitated [that they undergo] many reincarnations to "refine" and "whiten"[6] them. (Sha'ar HaPesukim, Shemos, "Vayakam Melech Chadash")

Though these souls originated from the same location in the sefiros as that of Moshe Rabbeinu, they entered the world spiritually blemished because of the manner in which they were created. It would take many reincarnations to rectify them, as it is explained:

---

[5] These are body-less souls that would be considered to be damaging spirits and demons.
[6] That is, to spiritually rectify them.

The beginning of their reincarnations was in the generation of the Flood. Since they were from this bitter root, having come out as wasted seed of the "Plague of Adam HaRishon," they rebelled against and denied God . . . (Sha'ar HaPesukim, Parashas Shemos, "Vayakam Melech Chadash")

The first reincarnation of these damaged souls was in the Generation of the Flood. They angered God, so He drowned them. Then, as the Arizal continues, they reincarnated into the next generation of the Tower of Bavel and united against God, so He dispersed them. Some then moved to Sdom and provoked God again, so He destroyed them.

It was in the next reincarnation, the fourth, that these souls divided into two groups:

All the souls that were rectified completely reincarnated into the Children of Israel and they were from the generation that went down to Egypt. There were souls that were not rectified and they became Egyptians, so Yosef had them circumcised, as it says in the verse, "Go to Yosef and do whatever he tells you to do" (Bereishis 41:55)[7] . . . Ya'akov his father also made many converts in Egypt

---

[7] Apparently Yosef was aware of these souls and their need for rectification and used his position as viceroy of Egypt and the famine as an opportunity to have the Egyptians perform circumcision, which allowed the future Erev Rav to emerge.

(Bereishis Rabbah 84:4). Those who converted and performed circumcision lived separate from the rest of Egyptian society and stood out among the rest of the Egyptians. (Sha'ar HaPesukim, Parashas Shemos, "Vayakam Melech Chadash")

Thus was born the Erev Rav, not in Moshe Rabbeinu's time, but in the time of Yosef HaTzaddik and Ya'akov Avinu. Though they helped in the process of rectifying these souls as well,[8] apparently it is Moshe Rabbeinu, whose soul originated from the same level as that of the Erev Rav,[9] who is principally responsible for their tikun.

There was more to Moshe Rabbeinu than Hevel and Shais however:

> After that the Neshamah [of Hevel] reincarnated in Moshe Rabbeinu, a"h. Since it never contained any element of evil, as mentioned above ... it says regarding him, "She saw that he was good" (Shemos 2:2). This excludes the Nefesh and Ruach which had good mixed together with evil. (Sha'ar HaGilgulim, Introduction 29)

Both the Nefesh and Ruach of Hevel were a

---

[8] This is why, the Arizal points out, that Ya'akov Avinu came down to Egypt at the age of 130.
[9] As the Arizal and the GR"A both point out, the gematria of "Erev Rav" is equal to that of "Da'as," the level of sefirah from which the soul of Moshe Rabbeinu and those of the Erev Rav came.

mixture of good and evil, and had to reincarnate, detailed in Sha'ar HaGilgulim, to separate out the evil from them until only good remained. Only the Neshamah had been purely good from the start, and this reincarnated into Moshe Rabbeinu. This is the sod of what it says regarding his birth: "She saw that he was good" (Shemos 2:2).

> It is already known that . . . the Ruach will not come [to a person] until the Nefesh is completely rectified. Likewise, the Neshamah will not come until the Ruach is rectified . . . [Since] the Neshamah of Moshe was [already] rectified, his Nefesh and Ruach, which were already rectified as mentioned, could come [together with the Neshamah] in him. (Sha'ar HaGilgulim, Introduction 29)

As explained at the beginning of Sha'ar HaGilgulim, one of the rules of reincarnation is that a rectified level of soul will not return with an unrectified level of soul. Even though the soul in need of rectification is on a higher level than the one that has been rectified, it is unacceptable for an "impure" level of soul to be together with one that has already been "purified."

By the time Moshe Rabbeinu was born however, the Nefesh and Ruach of Hevel had already reincarnated several times and achieved rectification. Furthermore, as mentioned, the Neshamah of Hevel was rectified from the beginning, so it could reincarnate directly into Moshe Rabbeinu the first time, together with the rectified Nefesh and Ruach. Moshe Rabbeinu was born already completely rectified.

> Hence, all the levels of reincarnation are hinted to in the following manner. The Shin of "Shais" is in [in the name] "Moshe," [as well as] the two letters of Shin-Mem [from "Shem," the son of Noach]. All of them are in "Moshe," as well as the Heh of "Hevel" . . . (Sha'ar HaGilgulim, Introduction 29)

"Moshe" is spelled, Mem-Shin-Heh. The letter Shin alludes to Shais whose name is spelled, Shin-Tav, and from whom the Nefesh of Hevel reincarnated before coming to Moshe Rabbeinu. Both the Shin and the Mem allude to "Shem" through whom the Ruach of Hevel reincarnated for the sake of tikun before coming to Moshe. The Heh of "Moshe" hints to Hevel—Heh-Bais-Lamed—himself, the source of all three levels of soul.

> With this [explanation] the verse, "And You said, 'I shall know you by name' " (Shemos 33:12) can be understood, because we don't find this conversation mentioned in any verse. (Sha'ar HaGilgulim, Introduction 29)

Yearly this verse is read by countless Jews, but rarely do people wonder to what it refers. When did God tell Moshe Rabbeinu, "I know you by name," and why is it not mentioned in the

Torah itself? As a result, Sod has a deeper explanation for Moshe's statement: it is an allusion to the fact that he is also the reincarnation of Shem.

> Noach also reincarnated into him, hinted to by the words, "and you have found favor in My eyes" (Shemos 33:12), which is "Noach" backwards. (Sha'ar HaGilgulim, Introduction 29)

Thus, not only did Shais, the son of Adam HaRishon and Shem, the son of Noach, reincarnate into Moshe Rabbeinu, but Noach did as well. This is alluded to by the Hebrew word for "favor," which is "chayn" and is spelled Ches-Nun, the reverse spelling of "Noach."

At the end of Moshe's life, which is also the end of the Torah, testimony is given to the greatness of Moshe Rabbeinu. It says:

> There was no other prophet who arose in Israel like Moshe, whom God knew face to face, as manifested by all the signs and wonders which God had sent him to perform in the land of Egypt, to Pharaoh and all his servants, and to all his land and all the strong hand, and all the great awe, which Moshe performed before the eyes of all Israel. (Devarim 34:10-12)

On a simple level this refers only to his original lifetime, the one recorded in the Torah. Once upon a time Moshe was a great prophet, greater than any prophet that ever came after him. Being prophecy, the Torah can know such information in advance.

On the level of Sod, it is a different, deeper story, as it says in Sha'ar HaGilgulim:

> The matter is as it says in the Book of the Zohar in Raya Mehemna, that Moshe Rabbeinu, a"h, had been the teacher of the entire Jewish people, and his interpreter had been Aharon HaKohen, as it says, "He will be a mouth for you" (Shemos 4:16), because Moshe had a "heavy" mouth and a "heavy" tongue. At the End-of-Days, in the generation of Moshiach in which Moshe will reincarnate and [once again] teach Torah to the Jewish people, he will also be of "uncircumcised lips." (Sha'ar HaGilgulim, Introduction 36)

Not only does Moshe Rabbeinu reincarnate as Moshiach to complete his role as redeemer of the Jewish people, he will also resume his position as the greatest prophet and teacher that ever lived. No one can surpass him as a prophet, even the great ones who arose throughout the millennia of history since his death. Only Moshe Rabbeinu can surpass himself, when he returns as teacher of the Jewish people once again.

By then it will be an entirely different period of history. And, even though the nation at the end of history is supposed to have the souls of the nation from the beginning of history, as it says:

> There is not a single generation in which
> Moshe Rabbeinu, a"h, is not there . . . in order
> to rectify [each] generation. Also, the Gener-
> ation of the Desert itself with the Mixed Mul-
> titude will reincarnate in the final generation,
> "like in the days of leaving Egypt" (Michah
> 7:15). (Sha'ar HaGilgulim, Ch. 20)

it will be after all the refinement and whitening of
history and Torah. They will have the same souls
but they will be on an entirely different spiritual
level.

The same, therefore, will be true of Moshe
Rabbeinu. Though he was born with all three levels of soul already rectified, he will be able to attain
even higher levels of soul. What he told the Jewish
people just before he died:

> God was angry with me because of you, and
> He did not listen to me . . . (Devarim 3:26)

will no longer apply. There will no longer be anything or anyone to hold him back from reaching
the highest levels possible.

ten
otherfamous
gilgulim

ELIEZER WAS AVRAHAM'S Avinu's trusted servant. He didn't only manage Avraham's household,[1] a spiritual matter as well as an organizational one. He was even trusted with one of the most sacred missions of all: find the soul mate of Yitzchak.[2]

Eliezer was also a Canaanite. This is why, as much as Avraham Avinu trusted him, he could not permit Yitzchak to marry his daughter, as Eliezer had hoped, even dreamed.[3] Yitzchak descended from Shem whom Noach had blessed, while Eliezer was a descendant of Canaan, whom Noach had

---

[1] Bereishis 15:2.
[2] Bereishis 24:1.
[3] Bereishis Rabbah 59:12.

cursed.[4] It was not right that one who was blessed marry one who is cursed.

Eliezer had no choice but to accept his master's decision, which he did with equanimity, as he left for Charan, Mesopotamia, to find a wife for Yitzchak from Avraham's family. What he did not know when he set out on his journey was that it would end up being a personal one as well, from the spiritual category of "Cursed" to that of "Blessed," as it says:

> Know that Eliezer, the servant of Avraham, was included in the curse of Canaan, but "entered" the category of "Blessed" when Lavan said to him, "Come blessed of God" (Bereishis 24:31), as Chazal say. (Sha'ar HaGilgulim, Introduction 36)

Lavan, the brother of Rivkah, did not have a great reputation. In the Torah he is a cheat and he might have later become a murderer had not God intervened on behalf of Ya'akov Avinu, his nephew and son-in-law. In short, he was one the least likely people to be the reason for someone as righteous as Eliezer to become spiritually transformed for the better.

Nevertheless, what seems like a simple welcome to the home of Besuel, the father of Rivkah and Lavan, was in fact Eliezer's rite of passage to the realm of the "Blessed." And though this did not

---

[4] Bereishis 9:25.

mean that Eliezer's daughter could marry
Yitzchak any more than she could prior to the
transformation, it did mean something fantastic
for Eliezer himself:

> Since Lavan caused Eliezer to become recti-
> fied, he reincarnated into Caleiv, the son of
> Yefuneh. This is why he is called "son of Yefu-
> neh," [to indicate that Caleiv was] the "son"
> of Lavan, as it writes regarding him, "I have
> cleared the house" (Bereishis 24:31). He is
> considered like his son since he entered him
> into the category of "Blessed," and he became
> rectified and reincarnated into Caleiv be-
> cause of his blessing. (Sha'ar HaGilgulim, In-
> troduction 36)

The first time Caleiv appears in the Torah is
as one of the 12 spies sent to investigate Eretz Yisroel in advance of the arrival of the rest of the nation.[5] He became a hero as one of the only two
spies to speak favorably about making aliyah, es-
caped the Divine decree that killed off the rest of
his generation in the desert, and merited to enter
the land under Yehoshua bin Nun after Moshe
Rabbeinu's death.

There is no indication in the Torah that there
was anything special about Caleiv, not in the
present and not in the past, with the exception of
one hint:

---

[5] Bamidbar 13:6.

[In actuality] Caleiv was the son of Chetzron, and not the son of Yefuneh. It is because of this question [about the name change] that our rabbis, z"l, have mentioned another elucidation, that [the name "Yefuneh" alludes to how] he "turned away" from the conspiracy of the Spies. (Sha'ar HaGilgulim, Introduction 36)

The Hebrew word that is the basis of the name "Yefuneh" means to "turn away." This, the rabbis say, was to indicate that Caleiv turned away from the plan of the spies. It is more a statement of fact than a revelation since the Torah itself discusses this.

On the level of Sod, it is a revelation. Kabbalistically, it is an allusion to the source of Caleiv's gilgul, that he came from Eliezer, the trusted servant of Avraham. The word "yefuneh" can also mean "clear away," something Lavan did for Eliezer who would not stay in a place that was filled with idols.

With this insight, another detail from the story of the Spies takes on added meaning. It says:

They went up in the south and he came to Chevron ... (Bamidbar 13:22)

Caleiv went there alone to prostrate himself on the graves of the Avos [in prayer] that he not be enticed by his colleagues to be part of their counsel. (Rashi)

The logic behind this is sound. It becomes even more profound after learning the following:

> Since Caleiv was the level of Eliezer, servant of Avraham, it writes about him that "he came to Chevron" (Bamidbar 13:22). Our rabbis, z"l, say that he went to prostrate himself on the graves of the Forefathers, because Avraham was the leader of them and he had once been his servant. Therefore at that time he went there [to pray for assistance]. (Sha'ar HaGilgulim, Introduction 36)

As Caleiv, he simply went to Chevron because it was the place of his ancestors to invoke their help to withstand the pressure to capitulate to the evil plan of his fellow spies. As the reincarnation of Eliezer, he went to his master's burial place and invoked assistance from the one he had always served so loyally. Apparently, it worked.

It does not mention from whom Yehoshua reincarnated. It does mention however that the Yud which Moshe attached to his name to change it from "Hoshea" to "Yehoshua" was also a "reincarnation." It was the same Yud, according to the Midrash, that was removed from "Sarai," the name of the wife of Avraham Avinu, to make it "Sarah."[6]

---

[6] Bereishis Rabbah 47:1. After complaining to God about being removed the name of such a righteous person, God told it that it would become part of the name of another very important person in the future.

Thus, while Avraham saved Caleiv from the plot and fate of the 10 dissenting spies, Sarah did the same for Yehoshua.

❖Lavan, Bilaam, and Naval HaCarmelli

Eliezer wasn't the only one to benefit from Lavan's welcome greeting. Lavan himself was also transformed by his own blessing:

> Since Lavan merited this level to remove him[7] from the category of "Cursed," he was also rectified and reincarnated into Naval HaCarmelli, and the two of them were the reincarnations of Bilaam, as has been explained. (Sha'ar HaGilgulim, Introduction 36)

Lavan lived in Ya'akov Avinu's time. Bilaam was a sorcerer in the time of Moshe Rabbeinu. Naval HaCarmelli was the one who cursed Dovid HaMelech.[8] Physically they were three very different people, but one soul gave each of them life and made them who they were, and is the basis of valuable insights into the life of each.

For example, after Lavan caught up to a fleeing Ya'akov Avinu, they made a pact to never come and do harm to the other. To memorialize their agreement, the Torah says:

So Ya'akov took a stone and set it up [as] a

---

[7] That is, Eliezer.
[8] I Shmuel 25:1.

monument. And Ya'akov said to his kinsmen, "Gather stones," and they took stones and made a pile, and they ate there by the pile. And Lavan called it "Yegar Sahadusa," but Ya'akov called it "Gal Eid." (Bereishis 31:45-47)

The names mean the same thing, "Pile of Testimony," except that Lavan named the monument in his native tongue of Aramaic, while Ya'akov used his, which was Hebrew. According to both, it was to act as reminder to either of them who might be on their way to do harm to the other.

The death of either Ya'akov or Lavan should have rendered the monument useless. Certainly the death of the both of them would have made the "Pile of Testimony" nothing more than a historic relic, a reminder of a death-defying crisis in the past. It would be significant but not active, which is why Gal Eid does not show up again anywhere in the Torah.

Not exactly. Fast-forwarding to a time period long beyond the lives of both Ya'akov and Lavan, when the descendants of Ya'akov Avinu are about to enter their promised land, the Torah introduces Bilaam, the evil sorcerer. He has been contracted by Balak, the king of Moav to curse the Jewish people because, as Balak says:

". . . for I know that whomever you bless is blessed and whomever you curse is cursed." (Bamidbar 22:6)

The Talmud explains the basis of Bilaam's ability to curse people, at least on a Pshat level.[9] On the level of Sod, however, if Bilaam is the reincarnation of Lavan who, as explained previously, had ability to bless people, this would also give him the supernatural ability to curse people as well.

The Lavan-Bilaam connection provides an interesting insight into another detail of the story:

> The she-donkey saw the angel of God stationed on the road with his sword drawn in his hand, so the she-donkey turned aside from the road and went into a field. Bilaam beat the she-donkey to get it back onto the road. The angel of God stood in a path of the vineyards, with a fence on this side and a fence on that side. The she-donkey saw the angel of God, and she was pressed against the wall. She pressed Bilaam's leg against the wall, and he beat her again. (Bamidbar 22:23-25)

There does not seem to be very much that is unusual about this, at least from a Torah perspective. The angel was sent to confront Bilaam while he passed between two walls to limit the movement of the donkey. This way Bilaam's leg could be trapped and he would become angry, setting up his eventual humiliation.

Kabbalistically there is a deeper message:

---

[9] Avodah Zarah 4b.

> The angel of God stood in a path of the vineyards, with a fence—gahder—on this side and a fence—gahder—on that side. (Bamidbar 22:24)

> Unless specified otherwise, [the Hebrew word] "gahder" refers to [a fence] made of stone. (Rashi)

Even if true, what essential piece of information does Rashi add with his comment? Rashi is indicating that the angel came to block Bilaam at this precise location because it was the location of Gal Eid, the mound of stones set up by Ya'akov and Lavan precisely to prevent Bilaam from doing what he intended to do, harm the descendants of Ya'akov.[10]

After all, God had already given Bilaam permission to accompany the messengers of Balak back to Moav, as it says:

> God came to Bilaam at night and said to him, "If these men have come to call for you, arise and go with them, but the word I speak to you, that you shall do." (Bamidbar 22:20)

This would seem to make the visit by the angel superfluous. If, however, Bilaam was passing Gal Eid to do harm to Ya'akov, then the angel had a different purpose. He had come to remind Bi-

---

[10] The Tosefes Berachah (Boruch HaLevi Epstein, 1860–1941).

laam that his mission was further complicated by the oath he had made to Ya'akov back in his days as Lavan.

Apparently it didn't work. Instead, Bilaam with his bloated personality continued on with his mission, and though not completely successful he did inflict significant damage on the Jewish people in a place called Shittim. Consequently he paid his own price for this, ironically while in Midian collecting his fee for his advice. When the Jewish people exacted revenge against Midian for their role, Bilaam was killed as well. He died around 34 years of age.[11]

After that, the only mention of Bilaam in the Torah is in reference to what he once tried to do. There is no indication, on a Pshat level, that he returned in any shape or form. That information belongs to the realm of Sod:

> Bilaam the Evil, who was a snake charmer, only had power in his mouth and was able to curse people effectively. Thus when Bilaam was killed he reincarnated into a single rock, the level of inanimate, to atone for the snake charming he did with his mouth, as mentioned. When he reincarnated after that it was into Naval HaCarmelli, which was the beginning of his return to this world to become rectified. (Sha'ar HaGilgulim, Introduction 22)

---

[11] Sanhedrin 106b.

Bilaam died in the year 2488, or 1272 BCE, the last of the 40 years of Jewish desert wandering. Dovid HaMelech was not king of the Jewish people until 2884, or 876 BCE, 396 years later, the same year that Naval cursed Dovid HaMelech, as the story says:

> There was a man in Maon, whose possessions were in Carmel. And the man was very great, and he had 3,000 sheep and 1,000 goats; and he was, while shearing his sheep, in Carmel. The man's name was Naval, and his wife's name was Avigayil . . . Dovid heard in the desert that Naval was shearing his sheep. And Dovid sent ten youths, and Dovid said to the youths, "Go up to Carmel, and you shall come to Naval, and greet him in my name. And you shall say, 'So shall you be living next year, and may peace be to you, and peace to your household, and peace to all that is yours. And now, I have heard that they are shearing for you. Now, your shepherds were with us. We did not disgrace them, neither was anything missing to them all the time they were in Carmel. Ask your youths and they will tell you, and may the youths find favor in your eyes, for we have come on a festive day. Give now, what your hand will find, for your servants and for your son Dovid.' " And Dovid's youths came and spoke to Naval according to all these words in Dovid's name, and they rested. Naval answered Dovid's ser-

vants and said, "Who is Dovid and who is Ben Yishai? Nowadays, there are many slaves, who break away, each one from his master." (I Shmuel 25:2-10)

Needless to say, Naval's words were not well received by Dovid and he decided to take him to task for them. On a God level though, it was not only because of the unfair treatment he gave Dovid HaMelech at that time. Apparently Dovid was aware of the deeper significance of Naval's harsh treatment:

> When the incident occurred in which he angered Dovid and said, "Who is Dovid and who is Ben Yishai?" (I Shmuel 25:10), Dovid wanted to kill him since he had come to rectify the evil speech of Bilaam and instead sinned more by again transgressing with his mouth, cursing Dovid, the king of Israel. (Sha'ar HaGilgulim, Introduction 22)

Thus, Dovid would have killed Naval had not Avigayil interceded on her husband's behalf, who had been drinking the night before. When Naval's wine wore off the next day and she told him what she had done, it says:

> It was in the morning, when the wine had left Naval, that his wife told him these things, and his heart died within him, and he became like stone. It was just ten days after that God in-

flicted a stroke on Naval, and he died. (I Shmuel 25:37-38)

From the sound of it, Naval became upset because his wife had gone behind his back to be kind to the man he had rejected and cursed. On a deeper level, it says:

> Then Naval remembered, and knew that in the beginning he had reincarnated into a rock to rectify the evil speech of Bilaam, and that now he had cursed again. Therefore "his heart died within him" when he remembered that he had originally been a rock to become rectified, as mentioned. (Sha'ar HaGilgulim, Introduction 22)

What ultimately disturbed Naval, therefore, was not what his wife had done without his knowledge, but what he himself had done, with his knowledge.

> Therefore, it does not write, "and he became [a rock]," but rather, "he was a rock." (Sha'ar HaGilgulim, Introduction 22)

Being specific, it turns out that even the verse alludes to its Kabbalistic meaning. Had it only said that "he became like a rock," the implication would have been that he became this way only in reaction to the events that had occurred. The words, "he was a rock" implied that he had once been a rock, and that the events served to remind him of this.[12]

With the death of Naval, the soul of Lavan does not make any more appearances in history, at least none that are revealed in Sha'ar HaGilgulim.

❖More Recent Gilgulim

"Tannaim" is the name used to refer to the generations that authored the Mishnah.[13] It actually covers many generations that spanned a period of 530 years, from 310 BCE–220 CE. Regarding one Tanna, **Babba ben Buta,** the Talmud relates the following story:

> "Who are they," [Herod] asked, "who teach, 'From the midst of your brothers you shall set up a king over you' (Devarim 17:15)? The Rabbis!"[14] He therefore killed all of the rabbis, sparing only Babba ben Buta, so he could take counsel of him. He placed on his head a garland of hedgehog bristles and put out his eyes. (Bava Basra 3b)

---

[12] Rav Chaim Vital adds: Naval was an important person, so it doesn't have to be asked how he knew this. It is possible that a prophet or scholar told him, and it is possible that his mazal saw even though he did not see (Sha'ar HaGilgulim, Introduction 22).

[13] The short and concise teachings of the oral portion of the Torah that are the basis of most Talmudic discussions.

[14] Herod had been a gentile servant who rebelled and took over the kingdom. The verse makes him unfit to be king over the Jewish people.

Herod lived between 73-4 BCE, and this overlapped with the life of Babba ben Buta, whom Herod had blinded. **Rav Sheishes** belonged to the next era of Torah scholars, the Amorayim (220-590 CE) who authored and edited the Talmud. According to the Arizal, Rav Sheishes was the gilgul of Babba ben Buta, which is why he was blind as well.[15] Even their names are the same in Gematria As-Bash.[16]

One of the most famous Tannaim is **Rebi Akiva,** regarding whom Moshe Rabbeinu himself told God:

> "You have someone such as him and You give the Torah through me?" (Menachos 29b)

There are many stories told about the great Rebi Akiva, who lived until 120 years but who died brutally at the hands of the Romans as one of the Ten Martyrs while saying the "Shema."[17] The journey of his soul, however, is less known:

> After Reuven repented he merited to bring the duda'im, which were the reason for the birth of Yissachar who was from the side of

---

[15] Sha'ar HaGilgulim, Introduction 4.

[16] One form of gematria divides the Aleph Bais in two and matches the last letter with the first one (Aleph-Tav), the second last letter with the second letter (Bais-Shin), etc. Hence the name "As-Bash," which is spelled Aleph-Tav, Bais-Shin. Therefore, the Bais-Bais of "Babba" corresponds to the Shin-Shin of "Sheishes," and the Aleph corresponds to the Tav.

[17] Brochos 61b.

good of Kayin the firstborn. Thus Chava said when Kayin was born, "I have acquired a man with God" (Bereishis 4:1), to hint [to Kayin's rectification through Yissachar] . . . She hinted to say that the complete rectification of Kayin would come through Yissachar, who was born as a result of the acquisition when Leah "purchased" Ya'akov from Rachel with the duda'im, as it says, "because I have hired you with my son's duda'im," (Bereishis 30:16). Thus this son was born, the portion of God from the side of good which was Yissachar . . . (Sha'ar HaGilgulim, Introduction 33)

Yissachar was the fifth son born to Ya'akov Avinu and Leah. He was conceived the night after Leah "purchased" the right to be with Ya'akov from Rachel.

The Torah relates how Reuven, Leah's first son, brought some wild flowers, duda'im, home for his mother. Rachel saw this and requested the flowers for herself, even offering to purchase them by giving up her opportunity to be with Ya'akov that night. Leah consented and informed Ya'akov of the "deal," from which Yissachar was conceived.

It is not clear from the Torah why Rachel insisted on Reuven's flowers for herself, or why she was prepared to sacrifice an opportunity to have a child from Ya'akov Avinu for which she lived. That requires the Midrash and Sod to explain, which makes the connection between the "acquisition" involved in the birth of Yissachar, and the one which resulted in the birth of Kayin, of whom Yissachar was both a reincarnation and rectification.

> Therefore, Eisav, who is the snake, had a hold on them, and the heel is called "Eisav" . . . (Sha'ar HaGilgulim, Introduction 33)

The snake to which this refers is the original one that tempted Chava into eating from the Aitz HaDa'as Tov v'Ra—the Tree of Knowledge of Good and Evil. As such the snake represents the yetzer hara, man's evil inclination, which has an innate connection to the concept of the "heel," as it says:

> God said to the snake, "Because you have done this, you are cursed more than all the cattle and more than all the beasts of the field. You shall walk on your belly and you shall eat dust all the days of your life. I will place hatred between you and between the woman, and between your seed and between her seed. He will crush your head, and you will bite his heel." (Bereishis 3:14-15)

The yetzer hara is also connected to the Sitra Achra,[18] the Satan, which is the ministering angel of Eisav as well.[19] Therefore, there is a direct connection between the snake and Eisav, which gave

---

[18] Bava Basra 16a.
[19] Midrash Tanchuma, Vayishlach 8.

him control over the spiritual level of "heel" since the sin of eating from the Aitz HaDa'as Tov v'Ra. This level corresponds to the level of Asiyah, Rabbi Vital explains, because it is so close to and accessible to the Klipos.

This is the way the situation remained until the actual birth of Ya'akov and Eisav, at which time.

> Ya'akov "grabbed" them from Eisav, b'sod, "His hand was holding onto the heel of Eisav" (Bereishis 25:26). After that, Yissachar was born from this level . . . (Sha'ar HaGilgulim, Introduction 33)

The significance of Ya'akov being born holding onto the heel of his twin brother Eisav is discussed in many places and on many levels. It is spiritually important enough that his own name, "Ya'akov," has the word "aikev—heel" built into it. This however adds another dimension to the discussion and explains how it prepared the way for the birth of Yissachar.

And not only Yissachar, because:

> After that, from the level of this heel, Rebi Akiva ben Yosef was born, named for this heel. (Sha'ar HaGilgulim, Introduction 33)

Just as the name "Ya'akov" has the letters of "aikev" in it, so does "Akiva." This was to indicate that Rebi Akiva was the reincarnation of Yissachar whose soul was the level of the "heel" after it had been recovered by Ya'akov Avinu from Eisav. It may have taken Rebi Akiva 40 years to enter the world of Torah, and an additional 24 years to become the great teacher of Israel that he became, but he was destined for greatness because of the soul with which he was born.

Rabbi Chaim Vital, author of Sha'ar HaGilgulim and foremost student of the Arizal, was from a much later time, living from 1542-1620, 78 years altogether. The story of his soul is one of the most interesting in the entire work.

It says:

> In the beginning I was the rabbi, HaRav Vidal dei Tulusa, the author of the work, "Maggid Mishneh," and his name was like mine is now. (Sha'ar HaGilgulim, Introduction 38)

Rabbi Vidal, which is like "Vital," wrote a commentary on the Rambam's Magnum opus called, "Yad Chazakah," otherwise known as the "Mishneh Torah." In this work, the Rambam synthesized the entire Talmud and codified all of its laws between 1170-1180 CE. He did, however, provide the reasons or the sources for many of his decisions, making the work highly controversial in its time.

This prompted Rabbi Vidal, who lived in the latter half of the 14th century, to write a running commentary on the entire Yad. He provided both explanations for the rulings of the Rambam and the Talmudic sources for his opinions. He called his commentary, therefore, "Maggid Mishneh," which literally means "speaker of the Mishneh."

> After, I reincarnated into a person whose name was Rebi Yehoshua Suriano, a very wealthy and elderly man who gave much charity. He would come early to, and leave late, from the synagogue and the study hall. After that I also reincarnated into someone whose name was "Avraham," a young boy 13 years old who died in his 14th year. (Sha'ar HaGilgulim, Introduction 38)

Rabbi Vital does not explain who these people were or any significance they may have had. He continues to say:

> [The Arizal] told me that the reason I had to reincarnate now was because of another reincarnation from the earlier ones, because I did not believe that much in the wisdom of the Zohar. From his words I understood that it was when I was in the reincarnation of the Maggid Mishneh . . . He told me that I need to rectify this now in this reincarnation, which means being involved with the wisdom of the Zohar. (Sha'ar HaGilgulim, Introduction 38)

The Zohar was not officially published until 1380 CE by Moshe de Leon. Until that time it was restricted to a small circle of Kabbalists, and even the Ramban, Rabbi Moshe ben Nachman (1194-1270 CE), did not believe in its teachings until later in life. It would take a while for Kabbalah to gain wider acceptance, and apparently Rabbi Vidal was one of those who dissented, focussing only the revealed and halachic parts of Torah tradition.

Rabbi Chaim Vital's life was just the opposite. His teacher was a master Kabbalistic and he was his foremost student. Revealed Torah was not as crucial to his development at this time, as the Arizal told him:

> He told me that when I was in the reincarnation of the author of the Maggid Mishneh I was an important investigator [of Torah matters] and sharp in the wisdom of in-depth study. Therefore I do not desire now to take the trouble for the wisdom of in-depth [investigation]. (Sha'ar HaGilgulim, Introduction 38)

The Arizal also revealed to his student iburim[20] that had come to him at difference points in his life, such Rebi Elazar ben Arach, the student of Rebi Yochanan ben Zakkai, and Rebi Elazar ben Shamua, the student of Rebi Akiva. Even Rebi Akiva himself at some point had been one of his iburim.

---

[20] Souls that come and join a person's own soul during parts of his or her life based upon merit.

It turns out however that the Maggid Mishneh was not the beginning of the story of Rabbi Vital's soul:

> My teacher . . . also told me on that day that my Nefesh has relevance and latches on to the Nefesh of Moshe Rabbeinu . . . I have a portion of the level of my Nefesh that is specifically from him . . . This Nefesh reincarnated after that many times, until it reincarnated into Rebi Yochanan ben Zakkai, and after that, into Rebi Akiva, and after that into many other reincarnations, until it reincarnated into Abaye, who was called "Nachmani," [and the] friend of Rava . . . After that this Nefesh was clothed in one of the Rabbanan Savorai, called Rav Achai . . . After that this Nefesh reincarnated into Rav Dustai Gaon, and after that several other reincarnations occurred, until it reincarnated into Rav Aharon HaLevi, the grandson of Rav Zerachiah HaLevi, the "Ba'al HaMaor." After that, he reincarnated into the author of the "Maggid Mishneh," then [into] Rebi Yehoshua Suriano, and after that into the young boy Avraham mentioned earlier. Later, he reincarnated into me, now, the young Chaim. (Sha'ar HaGilgulim, Introduction 38)

This is only part of the story, as Rabbi Vital explains. He reveals the sins that were committed by each of the people who preceded him, including the Maggid Mishneh, and how they had to reincarnate in him to rectify their sins. Perhaps one of the more amazing revelations is this note from Rabbi Chaim Vital's son, Rav Shmuel:

> He told me that during the time of the great teacher, z"l,[21] it was not possible at all to build Yerushalayim, but that during the time of my father and master, may he be remembered for eternal life, it would be possible if the Jewish people repented. Then my father and master, z"l, would have been Moshiach ben Yosef[22] . . . Thus I saw that my father, may he be remembered for eternal life, was quite afraid of the nations of the world, that they should not kill him . . . (Sha'ar HaGilgulim, Introduction 36)

As Rav Shmuel notes, and history confirms, this potential did not come to fruition, which he says was the result of the sins of the nation at that time. Instead Rabbi Chaim Vital died, but not without leaving behind personal manuscripts from the teachings of the most important Kabbalist of the last 500 years at least. They became the basis of the "Kisvei Arizal," one of the most important sources of Kabbalistic teachings ever.

---

[21] The Arizal.
[22] The Moshiach that precedes the final Moshiach, Moshiach Ben Dovid.

eleven
the ten martyrs

ONE OF THE most tragic but also heroic stories of all Jewish history is that of the Ten Martyrs. They were brutally murdered by the Romans for no reason other than being the righteous Torah leaders of their generation.

Today we recall them on Tisha B'Av and during the repetition of Mussaf on Yom Kippur, but once Moshe Rabbeinu was troubled by the death of Rebi Akiva and even questioned God about it,[1] as did the angels as well. According to the Talmud, the once great rabbi, Elisha ben Abuya, may have become a hectic because of the death of one of the martyrs.[2]

---

[1] Menachos 29b.
[2] Chullin 142b.

Something as major an occurrence as the death of ten of the greatest rabbis of all history has to have a reincarnation story as well. It does, alluded to by the unusual background provided in the Chazan's repetition of the Mussaf of Yom Kippur:

> These shall I recall and I pour out my soul within me, for wanton people have devoured me, as if I were an unturned cake. For in that ruler's[3] time there was no reprieve for the 10 who were murdered by the government. As [the ruler] studied the Book taught by the [Sanhedrin], which is likened to a nourishing heap [of wheat], he understood and analyzed the inscribed law. He opened it to, "These are the statutes" (Shemos 21:1), and thought of a plot based on [the verse], "If someone kidnaps a person and sells him, and he is found guilty, he is put to death." (Shemos 21:16). He became arrogant against the great [Sages] and ordered that his palace be filled with shoes, and sent for 10 great rabbis who plumbed the law and its principles through analytical discussion. [He commanded them:] "Judge this case authentically, and state the decision without perverted deceit. Rather, you must elucidate it truthfully and clearly: [What is the law] if a man is found to have kidnapped a member of his Jewish

---

[3] Hadrian.

brothers, and he enslaved him and sold him?"

They answered him, "The kidnapper is to die."

He said, "Then what about your ancestors who sold their brother, to a caravan of Arabs they peddled him and gave him away for shoes?"

The Roman referred to the kidnapping and sale of Yosef by his brothers.[4] The only question is, why? Romans never required an excuse to execute Jews, especially their Torah leaders. Why did the Roman leader feel the need to find one this time, and why specifically the story of the kidnapping of Yosef?

It was because though the Roman leader may have used the story as a pretext to martyr the rabbis, Hashgochah Pratis used it as the reason for their deaths. Many generations had come and gone since Yosef and his brothers, but the Ten Martyrs were directly connected to Yosef, and a specific event that occurred to him.

The Torah tells us about what happened to Yosef after he eventually ended up in Egypt. He was purchased as a slave by Potiphar, the chief butcher of Pharaoh. However, Divine Providence smiled down on Yosef and he quickly grew in responsibility and stature in the house of Potiphar.

He also caught the eye of his master's wife,

---

[4] Bereishis 37:20.

who became obsessed with Yosef to the point of adultery. He successfully rebuffed her on every occasion except for one:

> [And it came to pass about this time that] he went into the house to do his work.] There was none of the men of the house . . . (Bereishis 39:12)

> Was it possible that there was no man in a huge house like that of this wicked [Potiphar]! [Rather] it was taught in the School of Rebi Yishmael: That day was their festival, and they had all gone to their idolatrous temple. She pretended to be ill thinking, "I will not have an opportunity like today for Yosef to be with me."
> She caught him by his garment . . . (Bereishis 39:12)

> At that moment his father's image came and appeared to him through the window and said, "Yosef, your brothers will have their names inscribed upon the stones of the Ephod[5] and yours will be with theirs. Do you wish to have your name removed from among theirs and be called an associate of harlots?"

---

[5] The Ephod was an elaborate garment worn by the Kohen Gadol and upon which the Choshen containing the Urim v'Tumin rested (Shemos 28:6-14).

But his bow was strongly established . . . (Bereishis 49:24)

Rebi Yochanan said in the name of Rebi Meir, "[This means] that his passion subsided."
And his arms were gilded . . . (Bereishis 49:24)

He stuck his hands in the ground so that his lust came out from between his fingernails. (Sotah 36b)

No doubt this was a historically important incident, especially for Yosef and his future descendants. The test had the potential to reduce the number of Godly Tribes from 12 to 11, which would have been an unmitigated disaster for Ya'akov Avinu and the Jewish people in general. Why though should it be specifically connected to the death of the the Ten Martyrs?

The answer has to do with what happened to Yosef and what it meant to history. What exactly came out from between his fingernails?

All that happened to Yosef HaTzaddik in this world with the wife of his master Potiphar . . . likewise happened Above to the upper "Yosef HaTzaddik," the sefirah of Yesod. When the 10 . . . sparks of holy souls left the male upper Yesod and went to waste . . . the Klipos took these souls. (Sha'ar HaGilgulim, Introduction 26)

As the Vilna Gaon explains, whatever happened to Yosef was not physical.[6] Nothing physical could leave from his fingernails, but spiritual light could, and because it was emitted in an improper manner, it was taken by the Klipos.

Like most things of this nature that occur in the spiritual world there was an eventual impact on the physical world:

> The 10 Gevuros, five from Abba and five from Imma, are the level of the Ten Martyrs whose souls were clothed within these "lights." The five Gevuros of Abba were: Rebi Akiva, Rebi Shimon ben Gamliel, Rebi Yesheyvav Ha-Sofer, Rebi Yishmael ben Elisha Kohen Gadol, and Rebi Yehudah ben Babba. This seems to me to be the actual order, since Rebi Akiva was the Chesed within Gevuros, Rebi Shimon ben Gamliel was the Gevuros of the Gevuros, etc. . . . The rest of the soul clothing were the five remaining Martyrs, from the five Gevuros of Imma. Since the Ten Martyrs mentioned were clothing from the level of Gevuros and judgment, they needed to be killed because the Klipos cling the strongest to Gevuros, as it is known, [especially with such an improper emission of spiritual light] . . . (Sha'ar HaGilgulim, Introduction 26)

From a historical perspective, the Romans

---

[6] Biur HaGR"A, Tikunim, Tikun 69,

were just another empire bent on conquering the known world of their time. They were tech savvy and this gave them the ability to greatly increase their military might and easily conquer surrounding nations. Eretz Yisroel being just across the Mediterranean and the gateway to the Middle East was a high priority for any conquering nation.

The larger an empire the more it has to impose its will on its subjects. An empire as massive as the Roman Empire was costly to supervise and therefore it had to demand from its citizens a certain level of loyalty to its culture in order to keep people in line. Since most religions were pagan at that time, it was not hard to get people to switch to the Roman way of life.

The only real exception was the Jews. The weaker elements bowed to Roman pressure to convert, but the core of the Jewish people, the leading rabbis of that time, would not. This naturally put them on a collision course with the Romans who, always looking to make an example of the rebellious, were bound to capture and torture the "traitors" to death. Historically, this is the story of Asarah HaRugei HaMalchus—the Ten Martyrs.

Kabbalistically, that is only the cover story. The real reason of why the Ten Martyrs had to die went all the back to Yosef and the incident with the wife of Potiphar. What occurred that fateful day created the problem. Almost fifteen hundred years later it was rectified through the heroic deaths of the Ten Martyrs at the hands of the Romans. To appreciate why, the following must be understood:

> Know that there is not a soul in the world that can be, God forbid, bare without one [layer of] "clothing" in which it is clothed in this world . . . This clothing always clings to the souls, and this clothing does not ever separate from the soul within it, even after resurrection. (Sha'ar HaGilgulim, Introduction 26)

The clothing of the soul, unlike that of the body, is also completely spiritual. Though it does not come from the same source of the soul, it has a big impact on the destiny of a person. The spiritual reality of what came from Yosef resulted into the clothing over the souls of the Ten Martyrs, and determined their means of death. Because of the circumstances that led to the creation of this "clothing," a specific tikun was necessary that could only come through the terrible deaths of the Ten Martyrs.

This is why they had to be told to accept their judgment and with love. They could have used spiritual means to overturn the decree against them. However, the angel indicated to them that though this would have saved their lives it would not have dealt with the larger problem of rectifying the clothing of the souls, something history required for the ultimate purpose of Creation to be fulfilled.

It is an amazing thing when one considers the chain of events that resulted in the death of the Ten Martyrs. It started with Ya'akov's favoritism of Yosef and the jealousy it caused in his brothers.[7] This led them to sell their brother into slavery which brought him down to Egypt.

This however was only the catalyst to fulfill the prophecy given to Avraham Avinu, that his descendants would be "strangers in a land that is not theirs . . . for 400 years" (Bereishis 15:13). According to the Midrash, the entire episode of Yosef and his brothers was a set up just to set the prophecy in motion:

> Rav Yudan said, "The Holy One, Blessed is He, wanted to carry out the decree of, 'Know that you shall surely be (strangers)' (Bereishis 15:13), and therefore set it up that Ya'akov would love Yosef so that the brothers would hate him and sell him to the Arabs, and they would all go down to Egypt . . ." (Tanchuma, Vayaishev 4)

We know from Yosef's dreams that it was the Divine plan to have Yosef become viceroy over Egypt. What we did not know was that his path to

---

[7] Shabbos 10b.

leadership was via slavery in Egypt and a 10-year[8] prison sentence in an Egyptian jail. Somehow all of this was part of his preparation for becoming viceroy over the largest nation at that time.

Yosef could have gone to prison for a number of reasons, but it ended up being the result of the false accusations of adultery made against him by his master's wife. She had tried to tempt Yosef to sin, and his rejection of her made her into his enemy, landing him in jail.

We are told that Yosef brought this on himself. The attraction of the wife of Potiphar for her Jewish slave apparently was in response to Yosef's lack of sensitivity to the impact that his apparent death was having on his father:

> So he left all that he had in Yosef's hand, and he knew nothing about what was with him except the bread that he ate. Yosef had handsome features and a handsome appearance. (Bereishis 39:6)

> Yosef had handsome features: As soon as Yosef found himself [in the position of] ruler, he began eating and drinking and curling his hair. The Holy One, Blessed is He, said, "Your father is mourning and you curl your hair! I will incite the 'bear' against you." Immediate-

---

[8] Apparently Yosef was only supposed to be in jail for 10 years. Two years were added to his sentence because Yosef placed his trust in the Egyptian wine steward for redemption (Rashi, Bereishis 40:23).

ly afterwards "his master's wife lifted up her eyes." (Rashi)

Had the wife of Potiphar not set eyes on Yosef, something which was not very common for an Egyptian especially in her position to do, Yosef would never have considered her even for a moment. As loyal as he was to his master he was far more loyal to God.

Yet, she was attracted to Yosef, and apparently it was more than physical. According to the Midrash, her astrologers had predicted that she and Yosef would have common descendants which only encouraged her to pursue Yosef more. This told her that her desire for Yosef were sanctioned by Heaven.[9] It did not tell her that the common family line would come through her adopted daughter, Osnas, whom Yosef would later marry after becoming viceroy of Egypt.[10]

It sounds like the story of Yehudah and his daughter-in-law, Tamar, which happens to precede the story of Yosef and the wife of Potiphar in the Torah, perhaps for this reason as well. The Talmud says that Heaven guided Yehudah towards Tamar, seemingly because their union had to occur to produce Peretz, the ancestor of Dovid HaMelech.[11] Given the events that led to Yosef's test, it

---

[9] Bereishis Rabbah 85:3.
[10] She was the daughter from Dinah and Shechem. She was sent down to Egypt as a baby and adopted by Potiphar and his wife who could not have children (Pirkei d'Rebi Eliezer, Ch. 32).
[11] Sotah 10b.

seems as if he too was pushed by Hashgochah Pratis to undergo what he did.

The question is, how could such a positive outcome result in such a negative consequence? Clearly Yosef's success resulted in tremendous tikun for himself, and perhaps history as well. Why did it also result in a spiritual emission that became the soul clothing of the Ten Martyrs, and the cause of their tragic deaths?

There is actually an example of this very idea in the Talmud with respect to Adam HaRishon:

> Rebi Yirmiyah ben Elazar further stated: In all those years during which Adam was excommunicated he fathered Ruchin, Shiddin, and Lillin, as it says: "And Adam lived 130 years and fathered a son in his own likeness, after his own image" (Bereishis 5:3), from which it follows that until that time he did not father [someone] after his own image. (Eiruvin 18b)

As the Talmud indicates, for 130 years after being expelled from the Garden of Eden, Adam HaRishon did teshuvah. Part of his atonement process, the Talmud explains, included a spiritual purging that resulted in an unwelcome historical by-product:

All the shiddin and Ruchin[12] that Adam created during the 130 years that he separated from Chava were holy and elevated souls from the level of [the sefirah of] Da'as, [except] that [they came into the world] mixed together with the Klipos. This necessitated [that they undergo] many reincarnations to "re-fine" and "whiten"[13] them. (Sha'ar HaPesukim, Parashas Shemos, Vayakam Melech Chadash)

One could argue that this would not have been necessary had Adam HaRishon simply obeyed God and not eaten from the Aitz HaDa'as Tov v'Ra. However, the same Midrash quoted above begins with the following:

Go and see the works of God, awesome in deed toward mankind. (Tehillim 66:5)

Go and see how when The Holy One, Blessed is He, created the world, He created the Angel of Death on the first day as well . . . Man was created on the sixth day and yet death was blamed on him! To what is this similar? To a man who decided that he wanted to divorce his wife and wrote her a bill of divorce, after which he came home holding it, looking for a

---

[12] These are body-less souls considered to be damaging spirits and demons.
[13] That is, to spiritually rectify them.

pretext to give it to her. He told her, "Prepare me something to drink."

She did, and taking it he said [to her], "Here is your Get."[14]

She asked him, "Why?"

He told her, "Leave my house! You made me a warm drink!"

She said, "You were able to know [before coming home] that I would prepare you a warm drink that you wrote a bill of divorce in advance and came home with it?"

Adam said something similar to The Holy One, Blessed is He. "Master of the Universe! The Torah was with You for 2,000 years before You created the world . . . What is written in it, 'This is the law when a man will die in a tent' (Bamidbar 19:14). If You had not decided that Your creations should be able to die, would You have written this?! Yet You blame death on me!" (Tanchuma, Vayaishev 4)

The point that the Midrash is making that God does work in mysterious ways, though it is always for the good of man and Creation. The Talmud calls this "Kavshei d'Rachmana," the "Hidden Things of God,"[15] while the Midrash refers to it as, "Alillus," or "Pretext." Both terms refer to the historical events that occur but which do not make sense to us in a God-driven world.

---

[14] Halachic divorce document.
[15] Brochos 10a.

Kabbalah begins to unravel the mystery somewhat by referring to such historical anomalies as, "Mirmah u'Tachboles," literally, "Scheming and Trickery." It is a complicated idea, but simplified it refers to events that are necessary for the sake of the ultimate mandate of Creation when man himself lacks the merit to make them occur.[16] Thus it says:

> This is also the sod of the matter mentioned in the Midrash, "These I will recall" (printed in the book "Rav Pa'alim" and in the liturgy of the Yom Kippur Mussaf) regarding the Ten Martyrs. The Holy One, Blessed is He, said [to the angels], "If I hear another voice I will turn the world to null and void!" (Drushei Olam HaTohu, Chelek 2, Drush 4, Anaf 18, Siman 2)

According to the Talmud even the angels protested to God about the violent nature of Rebi Akiva's death.[17] In response God told them to remain silent or He would return the world to null and void, seemingly in anger to the impertinence of the angels.

The angels, however, had not been impertinent, and neither had God been angry. Rather, He was explaining to them why the Ten Martyrs had to die so cruelly:

---

[16] Sha'ar HaGilgulim, Introduction 38. See Session 7.
[17] Brochos 61b.

The returning of the world to null and void at that time [in history] . . . would have resulted in all of the rectification that was [instead] accomplished through the deaths [of the Ten Martyrs]. (Drushei Olam HaTohu, Chelek 2, Drush 4, Anaf 18, Siman 2)

From a secular point of view, the Romans were just another conquering power that left their mark on history. From a Divine perspective, the lifestyle they lived and exported to the rest of the world at that time was bringing Creation to a spiritual breaking point. Creation can cope with only so much sinning before a corrective measure must be taken.

This is because evil is a function of a spiritual force in Creation called "Gevurah," literally "Strength." When used properly the Gevuros are the basis of the kind of self-discipline that results in the performance of mitzvos and the avoidance of sin, both of which reveal God in Creation. It results in the kind of sanctification of God's Name achieved by the Ten Martyrs.

When used improperly the Gevuros cause sinning and the abuse of Creation. This in turn results in the concealing of God's Presence in Creation, a profanation of God's Name. This is contrary to the purpose of Creation and destructive to its existence, like cutting off the water supply to a tree.

Punishment turns the situation around. The suffering that punishment causes uses the Ge-

vuros in a corrective manner, resulting in a purging of sin and the "sweetening" of the Gevuros.
Thus, when any kind of destruction comes to Creation, it is to this end:

> All of the potential strength of the "judg-
> ments" would have been actualized through
> the destruction of the world, and it would
> have been complete "payment" for the entire
> world for all of their sins. This would have pu-
> rified the Gevuros from any [spiritual]
> "waste" and made them "holy to God" once
> again. (Drushei Olam HaTohu, Chelek 2,
> Drush 4, Anaf 18, Siman 2)

This puts into perspective the incredible historical significance of the martyrdom of these ten
great rabbis. Their deaths literally saved Creation,
being in place of the destruction of the world at
that time. As such, they were built into the primordial roots of Creation itself:

> All that occurred to the Ten Martyrs was
> prepared [in Creation] in the sod of the
> "World of Tohu" that existed prior to Cre-
> ation,[18] as God told Moshe Rabbeinu, a"h,
> "Silence! This is what went up before My
> mind!" (Menachos 29b), that is, they were
> prepared for all these grave deaths in order
> to complete the essential purpose of the null

---

[18] Bereishis 1:2.

[of Creation], which God intended for the sake of the future rectification. (Drushei Olam HaTohu, Chelek 2, Drush 4, Anaf 18, Siman 2)

When Moshe Rabbeinu questioned God about the death of Rebi Akiva,[19] God told him that Rebi Akiva's death fulfilled the mandate of Creation on an extremely high level of sefirah called "Machshavah," or "Mind." It was too high a level for even Moshe Rabbeinu to comprehend.

This is what God indicated to Moshe Rabbeinu when He responded, "Silence!" This indicated that the answer Moshe Rabbeinu sought could not be found on a level of human comprehension, and therefore was too sublime to be explained in words.

Had the Ten Martyrs not died the world would have been destroyed because of the sins of the generation, which were very strong and which made it impossible for the world to exist. (Drushei Olam HaTohu, Chelek 2, Drush 4, Anaf 18, Siman 2)

Thus, if anything, what happened to Yosef was a function of the null and void that exists within Creation and requires tikun. Likewise, his resistance to sin was also a tremendous act of Ge-

---

[19] While on Mt. Sinai, God gave Moshe Rabbeinu a future vision of Rebi Akiva, his teachings, and his death (Menachos 29b).

vuros, which brought about its own level of tikun as a result. At the same time it set in motion something that could be traced back to the primordial stages of Creation and which were essential to achieve the ultimate fulfillment of the purpose of Creation.

They were only ten rabbis, but because each one died as he did, heroically martyred at the hands of a cruel enemy, we are here today to know about it.

twelve
reincarnation & resurrection

ONE OF THE "Thirteen Principles of Faith" that many recite daily mentions the concept of Techiyas HaMeisim—the Resurrection of the Dead. Unlike reincarnation in which a soul returns in a new body that is born in another lifetime, resurrection is the return of the soul to an old body that has been recreated from its remains.

An example of this occurs in a prophecy:

> The hand of God was upon me, and God carried me out in a spirit, and set me down in the midst of the valley, and it was full of bones. He caused me to pass by them round about, and behold, there were very many in the open valley, and they were very dry. He said to me, "Son of man, can these bones live?"

I answered, "O God, You know."

Then He said to me, "Prophesy over these bones, and say to them, 'Dry bones! Hear the word of God!'"

Thus God said to these bones, "Behold, I will cause breath to enter into you, and you shall live! I will lay sinews upon you, and will bring up flesh upon you and cover you with skin, and put breath in you. You shall live, and you shall know that I am God."

So I prophesied as I was commanded, and as I prophesied, there was a noise, and behold a commotion, and the bones came together, bone to its bone. I looked, and there were sinews upon them, and flesh came up, and skin covered them above, but there was no breath in them. Then He said to me, "Prophesy to the breath, prophesy, son of man, and say to the breath, 'So says God, "Come from the four winds, O breath, and breathe upon these slain, so they may live."'"

So I prophesied as He commanded me, and the breath came into them, and they lived, and stood up upon their feet, an exceeding great host. (Yechezkel 37:1-10)

According to the Talmud these were not the bones of just any dead people. They were the bones of the people from the tribe of Ephraim who had left Egypt 30 years too early, and were slaughtered after leaving.[1] They died in 1343 BCE, and according to the Talmud were revived by Yechezkel the prophet[2] who did not live until the end of the First Temple period,[3] which was destroyed in 423 BCE.

The concept of resurrection is not difficult to understand. According to Kabbalah, it is the only way for man to finally rid himself of all the impurity that became a part of his being from his interaction with the original snake in the Garden of Eden:

> All those living will die in order to decompose the physicality of the body and to transform from Kasnos Ohr—AYIN-Vav-Raish—to Kasnos Ohr—ALEPH-Vav-Raish.[4] (Drushei Olam HaTohu, Chelek 2, Drush 4, Anaf 12, Siman 9)

One of the most dramatic impacts of our interaction with the snake was that mankind received a kind of indelible spiritual impurity called "zuhama." It was the reason for the transformation of man's skin from that of Divine light to that of the flesh we now have. As such man cannot enter the spiritual realm of the World-to-Come and therefore he must be transformed back to the pre-

---

[1] Shemos Rabbah 20:9. According to the Midrash, 300,000 from the Tribe of Ephraim were slaughtered by the Philistines.
[2] Sanhedrin 92b.
[3] Yechezkel prophesied from 434-423 BCE, over 900 years after the Tribe of Ephraim left Egypt early.
[4] The former means "light" and the latter means "skin" as we have now.

sin reality before going there after 6000. Techiyas HaMeisim will take care of this.

The question arises though, which body will resurrect? It was one soul that went from reincarnation to reincarnation, but each time it lived in a new body. If so, which of the many bodies that the soul inhabited will be the fortunate one to be resurrected at the end of history? Certainly one soul cannot resurrect in many bodies at the same time.

It doesn't have to. Instead, portions of a person's soul return in a body that was resurrected for it.

As explained previously, personal rectification takes place in stages. It is possible to become completely rectified in a single lifetime, but that is, for the most part, only in the first incarnation. For most people this is not the case necessitating reincarnation.

For example, a person may live out his entire life having only rectified a portion of his first level of soul, the Nefesh. By the time he dies, for example, only 40 percent of his Nefesh was rectified, requiring him to reincarnate to rectify the remaining 60 percent. If he fails to do this in his second lifetime then he will have to reincarnate again and again until his Nefesh is completely rectified.[5]

If, as per the example, the person rectified 40 percent of his Nefesh in his first lifetime, 40 percent more in his second lifetime, and the remain-

---

[5] Sha'ar HaGilgulim, Introduction 1.

ing 20 percent in his third lifetime, three bodies will need to resurrect. The first body after resurrecting will receive the 40 percent of the Nefesh that was rectified in its lifetime, the second body will receive the 40 percent that was rectified in it, while the third body will receive the remaining 20 percent.[6]

Therefore, during the period of resurrection many people will coexist possessing sections of the same soul. This is especially true since the rule of soul division is true for the levels of Ruach and Neshamah as well. The only difference is, it is explained, is that true spiritual enjoyment after resurrection will belong primarily to those bodies that receive levels of Ruach and Neshamah.

What happens to a person who commits sins for which the punishment is kares, and is therefore cut off from the Jewish people?[7] How does that affect the body and soul of a person who dies without having atoned for the sin that warrants such a punishment?

According to Sha'ar HaGilgulim, kares does not affect the soul as it does the body. It is the body that is completely destroyed in such a case, not the soul that was used to commit the sin. Consequently, the soul survives the body and therefore reincarnates into the next body, with which it will be associated in the future. At the time of resur-

---

[6] Sha'ar HaGilgulim, Introduction 4.
[7] The punishment for certain severe sins, such as eating forbidden fat or deliberately violating Shabbos without witnesses, is kares, or excision.

rection, this section of soul will return in the new body.

Thus, kares affects the body more than the soul. The soul will be impacted in as much as it will not be the main soul of the resurrected body in which it will reincarnate. This will limit the amount of pleasure a section of soul will have during that time.

According to the Zohar, the period of Techiyas HaMeisim is supposed to begin either in 2026, according to Rebi Yitzchak, or 2030, according to Rebi Yehudah. According to both opinions the entire period will last until the Jewish year 6000, or 2240 CE, at which time the world will transition to a higher plane of reality called "Olam HaBa," or the first stage of the "The World-to-Come."

Though the time from death to resurrection will be the same for everyone, not everyone will resurrect at the same time:

> It is logical to say that the time of decomposition of all those who die in advance of the resurrection will not be the same for everyone, but rather [will occur] for each person according to his [spiritual] level. (Drushei Olam HaTohu, Chelek 2, Drush 4, Anaf 12, Siman 9)

In other words, the time it will take for a body to decompose will vary from person to person: the more righteous a person was the less time it will take to decompose, being more spiritual. Since the point of decomposition is to eradicate the physicality of the body, and righteous people tend to be less materialistic, their bodies should require less time to become completely free of zuhama.

> However, according to another text in the Zohar mentioned, it says "and will resurrect us immediately," implying one time [of resurrection] for everyone. (Drushei Olam HaTohu, Chelek 2, Drush 4, Anaf 12, Siman 9)

This means that the amount of time it will take from burial until resurrection will be the same for everyone. If so, what difference will there be between the righteous person who controlled his desire for material pleasure and the people who overindulged in this world? The following:

> Nevertheless, it seems that the time of death and resurrection will vary for each person. Everyone will not die at the same moment which will cause the time of resurrection [for each person] to be different. For, someone who has previously become rectified from his zuhama will die and resurrect earlier, because death then will be only to decompose the physicality of the body, and to renew it. (Drushei Olam HaTohu, Chelek 2, Drush 4, Anaf 12, Siman 9)

This means that the entire period, either 210

or 214 years long, will consist of two kinds of people, those who have resurrected and those who have not. There will be people with Kasnos Ohr with an Ayin, that is, physical skin and a "normal" body, and those who with Kasnos Ohr with an Aleph, which is skin of light, a and far more spiritual body.

It is to this period of time that the Talmud refers when it states:

> Rebi Elazar said: There will come a time when "Holy" will be said before the righteous as it is said before The Holy One, Blessed is He. (Bava Basra 75b)

Which righteous people will be called "Holy"? Those who have already resurrected and look like Adam HaRishon before his sin. Who will call them this? Those who have yet to resurrect, and to whom the resurrected will appear like spiritual beings.

Kabbalah explains that as history continues to move forward even in Olam HaBa, the World-to-Come, Creation becomes increasingly more unified. The final state of tikun is called "Tikun Sod Achdus," which means "Rectification of the Mystery of Unity."[8] This will be a level of unification that is far too sublime to understand at this stage of history.

---

[8] Drushei Olam HaTohu, Chelek 2, Drush 3, Anaf 7; Sefer HaKlallim, Klal 17, Anaf 4, Os 11.

If so, then it might be assumed that even souls which have been divided among different bodies in Techiyas HaMeisim will eventually unify as well in later stages of Olam HaBa. This is something however that only God knows, as it says:

> Rebi Chiya ben Abba said in the name of Rebi Yochanan: All the prophets only prophesied for the days of Moshiach. As for the World-to-Come: "No one had ever heard, no ear had ever perceived, no eye had ever seen a god besides You perform for him who hoped for him" (Yeshayahu 64:3). (Brochos 34b)

In other words, at this time in history, only God knows what will transpire in the World-to-Come.

Nevertheless, Techiyas HaMeisim will not only be a significantly long period of time, it will be a time during which Creation, as we know it, will reach its full potential and perfection.[9] It will be Creation in its most ideal state. The collective pleasures of all lifetimes will pale compared to a single day of pleasure in this period of history, which will be yet a small fraction of the pleasure reserved for those going World-to-Come.

The point is that it is worth making material sacrifices now for spiritual gain then. It is important to limit the amount of reincarnating a person must do at this stage of history by achieving as much rectification as possible during any given

---

[9] Drushei Olam HaTohu, Chelek 2, Drush 3, Osios 1-4.

incarnation. This will minimize the amount of division that a level of soul will have to undergo, increasing its potential for pleasure after resurrection.

thirteen
achieving yabok

THE NAME "YABOK" should be a familiar one. It is the name of a northern tributary off the Jordan river. It became famous because it is the river by which Ya'akov Avinu confronted the angel and earning the name "Yisroel":

> [Ya'akov] got up that night and took his two wives, his two maidservants and his eleven children, and crossed over the Yabok crossing. He took them and all he owned across the river [and returned]. Ya'akov remained alone. A man wrestled with him until dawn, [but] when he wasn't able [to defeat Ya'akov], he touched the hollow of his hip. Ya'akov's hip socket became dislocated as a result of wrestling.

[The stranger] said, "Let me go! Dawn has arrived."

He answered, "I won't let you go unless you bless me."

He said to him, "What is your name?"

He answered, " 'Ya'akov'."

[The angel told] told him, "No longer will you be called 'Ya'akov', but 'Yisroel.' " (Bereishis 32:23-29)

However, that is where the importance of the river seems to end. In fact, it does not seem significant as a place for confrontation either, until a deeper meaning of the name is revealed. It may allude that there was, is, more to the name of the river than the Torah seems to indicate.

It says:

Know that if a man only performs mitzvos, [he only] merits the Nefesh called Asiyah,[1] but not more. He is similar to a woman whose husband has gone overseas and has left her unclothed, hungry and thirsty. It is like the Divine Presence that sits in exile; its house[2] destroyed it remains in exile in darkness. Thus is the Nefesh of a person while it lacks Ruach, its "husband," not having a source of light or intelligence to understand. (Sha'ar HaGilgulim, Introduction 18)

---

[1] That is, the Nefesh which comes from Asiyah.
[2] The Temple.

Of the 613 mitzvos in the Torah, 248 of them are positive mitzvos, commandments which tell a person to perform specific acts, liking saying the "Shema" twice a day, or to put on Tefillin. The rest are negative mitzvos, of which there are 365, which prohibit a person from performing certain acts, such as cooking milk together with meat, or performing forbidden activities on Shabbos.

Just completing the mitzvos in the proper manner is no simple task. Yet, if a person only does this he only gains access to the level of light of Asiyah, the lowest of the five worlds and source of the soul level of Nefesh.[3] On this level, he will live a very limited spiritual life, and will not be growth oriented. The person will spiritually stagnate and not be able to understand or appreciate the beauty of Torah and the opportunity for greatness it presents.

> If this person makes additional effort to learn Torah, learning, thinking about, and constantly teaching Oral Law, always learning Torah for its own sake, then he will merit the Ruach which is from Yetzirah. Then he will be like a woman whose husband has arrived, and who lives with her permanently in her house, clothing her, feeding her, and [giving her] drink . . . Such [will be] this person when the Ruach comes and will dwell within his Nefesh. Then his Nefesh will be filled with the

---

[3] See Session #2.

spirit of wisdom, and will ascend from Asiyah to Yetzirah. (Sha'ar HaGilgulim, Introduction 18)

As mentioned previously,[4] Torah is divided into two parts, Torah Sh'b'ksav—the Written Law —Torah Sh'b'al Peh—the Oral Law. The first part is the Torah scroll read weekly, and the second part is the basis of the Mishnah and Talmud learned in yeshivos for generations. It is the Oral Law that provides the necessary details for properly fulfilling the mitzvos mentioned in the Written Law.

It also corresponds to the next level of soul, Ruach. Learning Torah Sh'b'al Peh therefore gives a person access to this level of soul, and the more seriously he learns the Oral Law the higher the levels he will access. On such a level of soul a person becomes growth oriented and Torah becomes more than just an obligation. It becomes his lifeline and source of joy.

This however is not the end of his intellectual and spiritual journey, just the middle of it, if that:

If the person will make additional effort and learn Hidden Wisdom, the secrets of Torah, then he will also merit the Neshamah, which is from Beriyah. The Neshamah will give off light in the Ruach within him and will add a level to his level, wisdom to his wisdom, and he will then be called [a] "Complete Person,"

---

[4] See Session #1.

regarding whom it says: "God made man in His image" (Bereishis 1:27). (Sha'ar HaGilgulim, Introduction 18)

To many, the learning of Kabbalah is extraneous. It might be interesting, but even Torah scholars who have yet to learn it wonder about its relevance. For many generations, even its authenticity was in question.

Eventually it became clear that Sod is as much a part of the Torah tradition as those parts which were not in dispute.[5] This did not mean however that it was appreciated for what it means to spiritual growth. To this day most of the Torah world does not realize that without the learning of Kabbalah a person cannot fulfill his true spiritual potential.

The Torah sums up the creation of man in the following manner:

> God said, "Let us make man in our image, after our likeness, and they shall rule over the fish of the sea and over the fowl of the heaven and over the animals and over all the earth and over all the creeping things that creep upon the earth." And God made man in His image . . . (Bereishis 1:26-27)

The first man ever made was also the most perfect man. He was created in a very holy and

---

[5] See Session #1.

ideal state, which is why he was able to live in the Garden of Eden. It was his sin that changed all of this and made man what he is today, and why he was forced into exile from Paradise.[6]

It is virtually impossible to return to such a high level of existence prior to Techiyas HaMeisim, the Resurrection of the Dead.[7] Even people who are able to learn Sod do not return back to Adam's pre-sin state, and may look no different than those who only learn lower levels of Torah.

There is a spiritual difference however, even if there isn't a physical one at this stage of history. After all, if such growth was clearly visible to others it would compel them to learn Torah for this reason, and not because they have come to accept its Divine origin. The person himself who learns Sod will certainly experience the difference in level of completion, and the pleasure that accompanies it.

This is because Torah is more than knowledge. It is a pipeline for Divine light, and the higher the level of Torah learning, the higher the level of Divine light it can allow to flow a person. This in turn enhances a person's spiritual capacity and sensitivity, allowing them to sense and partake of correspondingly higher levels of existence.

Thus it says:

---

[6] Drushei Olam HaTohu, Drush Aitz HaChaim.
[7] See Session #12.

The sod of the matter is, when a person only has a Nefesh,[8] he does not receive Divine light[9] except from the Name [spelled] Aleph-Dalet-Nun-Yud[10] only. (Sha'ar HaGilgulim, Introduction 18)

There is only one God, but He has many Names, each referring to a particular manifestation of God in Creation. There are times when God works overtly in history, and times when He does so in a concealed manner. Sometimes God acts with mercy, but other times He is judgmental and acts strictly. There is a Name of God for each Divine manifestation or trait.

The general rule is that the more overt a revelation of God a Name represents, the holier it is. Thus, the Name of God that corresponds to His working through the "natural" world, which often gives people the impression that Creation is on "auto-pilot," is the one mentioned above and which is pronounced, "Adonai." This level of Divine light corresponds to the level of the Nefesh of Asiyah, and is too weak to inspire a person to do much more than maintain his spiritual status quo.

When he learns Torah for its own sake he also

---

[8] The Matok M'Dvash points out that the Nefesh, Ruach, and Neshamah mentioned here are all within the level of Asiyah itself, and not the general higher levels of Ruach and Neshamah.
[9] Divine light will flow to him on the level of this Divine Name only, limiting his spiritual ability.
[10] This Name corresponds to the level of Asiyah.

merits the Ruach which comes from the Name [spelled] Yud-Heh-Vav-Heh.[11] (Sha'ar HaGilgulim, Introduction 18)

This Name is called the "Shem Hovayah," since in non-Temple times it is too holy to be said the way it is written.[12] Nevertheless, when a person does more than simply perform mitzvos, learning Torah for its own sake, he gains access to the level of light to which this Name corresponds. His spiritual capacity enhanced, he can also access a higher level of soul—Ruach—and spiritually grow.

When he learns the secrets of Torah, he also merits Neshamah, and he will draw strength and Divine light from the Name [spelled] Aleph-Heh-Yud-Heh.[13] (Sha'ar HaGilgulim, Introduction 18)

Even though the level of Sod corresponds to the spiritual realm of Atzilus, the learning of it emanates light that results in access to the level of Beriyah and the soul level of Neshamah. This will give a person tremendous spiritual sensitivity which will give him more control over his physical

---

[11] God's four-letter Name which, during non-Temple times, is not pronounced the way it is written. This Name corresponds to the level of Yetzirah and the soul level of Ruach.

[12] Kiddushin 71a. "Hovayah" instead is spelled: Heh-Vav-Yud-Heh.

[13] Literally, "I will be what I will be" (Shemos 3:14), the answer that God told Moshe when he asked what to tell the people when they question him about who sent him.

reality, and a greater capacity to see and feel the reality of God in life.

More than this, when a person successfully reaches this stage of Torah learning, he also reaches a crucial threshold:

> When all three Names are joined together in a person they have the gematria of Yud-Bais-Kuf[14] and then it can be said of him, "God save! May the King answer us on the day we call!" (Tehillim 20:10), the initials[15] of which are Yud-Bais-Kuf. (Sha'ar HaGilgulim, Introduction 18)

Gematria, a division of Kabbalah, is more than just numerology. It is also a way to express a spiritual reality. When a person has accessed all three Names of God he is the recipient of their light and the levels of spiritual growth and personal completion they enable. This is represented by the total gematria of all three Names, which is 112, which can be written, Yud-Bais-Kuf, or "Yabok."

The number 112 can be represented by other combinations of Hebrew letters other than Yud-

---

[14] This spells the name "Yabok," the name of an eastern tributary of the Jordan river located about half-way between the Kinneret and the Dead Sea. Interestingly, this was the river that Ya'akov Avinu crossed with his family after leaving Lavan and at which he fought with the Angel of Eisav. After, his name was changed to Yisroel (Bereishis 32:23), and arriving at Shechem the Torah calls him shalim, or, complete (Bereishis 33:18).

[15] The first letter of the three last Hebrew words are Yud-Bais-Kuf.

Bais-Kuf. What is unique about these letters is that they themselves form a holy Name of God, one which incorporates two other Names, "Hovayah" and "Elohim."[16] It is also a Name alluded to by the Hebrew words "y'aneinu v'yom karaynu," which mean "answer us on the day we call!" as mentioned above.

Thus, the Name "Yabok" alludes to the spiritual completion of a person, his having reached the level called, "image of God." This may mean that the river Ya'akov Avinu crossed that fateful night before fighting the angel and earning the name, "Yisroel," was more significant than it seems. This is perhaps why it says shortly after:

> Ya'akov arrived complete at the city of Shechem. (Bereishis 33:18)

On a simple level, Rashi says that it means that he arrived at Shechem with his Torah, body, and money intact. On the level of Sod however, it means that having accessed his Nefesh, Ruach, and Neshamah, he had crossed his own personal "Yabok," and in the process reached the level of an Adam Shalaim.

---

[16] Sha'ar HaKavanos, Drush Kavanos Krias Shema, Drush 5.

four

dor hamidbar

THE GENERATION OF Jews that left Egypt under the leadership of Moshe Rabbeinu was called, "The Generation of the Desert," or "Dor HaMidbar" in Hebrew. They constituted but one-fifth, 3,000,000, of the total Jewish population in Egypt when the plagues began, as the Talmud,[1] Rashi,[2] and the Midrash point out:

> The four-fifths that died in the Plague of Darkness did so because they did not believe in the redemption. They acquired riches or held high positions in Egypt and did not want to leave. (Shemos Rabbah 14:3)

---

[1] Sanhedrin 111a.
[2] Rashi, Shemos 13:18; 10:22.

It was the remaining one-fifth that went to Mt. Sinai and received the Torah. Some 3,000 were lost after the incident of the golden calf,[3] but the rest left Mt. Sinai one year later for the Land of Canaan. Most of them would never make it.

Some more died soon after in a place called, "Kivros HaTa'avah," literally, "the burial places of the desire." It was called this because it was where they complained about the mann, and died as a result:

> The meat was still between their teeth. It was not yet finished, and the anger of God flared against the people, and God struck the people with a very mighty blow. (Bamidbar 11:33)

Even after this incident most of the one-fifth remained. It was the next sin that was catastrophic. It was the one which assured that almost every male, between the ages of 20 and 60 at that time, would die in the desert, even dig their own graves. It was their acceptance of exodus from Egypt that saved them during the Plague of Darkness. It was their rejection of aliyah to Eretz Yisroel that cost them their lives in the desert.

It was not the first time it happened. The Talmud says:

> Just as the coming to the Land was with two of the 60 myriads, so too was the leaving of

---

[3] Shemos 32:28.

Egypt with two of the 60 myriads. (San-hedrin 111a)

A "myriad" is equal to 10,000, so 60 myriads is equal to 600,000. The Talmud is saying that of the 600,000 males between the ages of 20 and 60 years that left Egypt and could have entered Eretz Yisroel,[4] only two actually did: Yehoshua bin Nun and Caleiv ben Yefuneh. The rest died off from one punishment or another over the course of the 40 years of desert wandering.

Likewise, the Talmud reveals that the same thing happened at the time of the exodus. Of the millions of Jews that could have left Egypt, there were 600,000 males between the ages of 20 and 60 years. Only two of them actually left, the rest dying during the Plague Darkness. This left men either younger than 20 years of age or older than 60 years, together with all of the females, to actually leave Egypt with Moshe Rabbeinu.

Tragic.

Catastrophic.

Ancient history.

Not entirely, as the Talmud concludes:

Rava said, "It will be likewise in Yemos HaMoshiach." (Sanhedrin 111a)

This means that at the time of the Final Re-

---

[4] It is to this particular group the number usually refers in the desert.

demption the situation will mirror what happened at the first redemption. Once again Jews will be required to leave the Diaspora for Eretz Yisroel, and once again the vast majority will choose to remain where they are. Only a small amount will actually survive the redemption, according to the Talmud.

The link between the two redemptions goes beyond the similar responses of many of the Jews at the time of both. In fact, though the Jews at the end of history are only physical descendants of the Jews from the beginning of Jewish history, they are more than this on the level of their souls:

> The Generation of the Desert itself with the Mixed Multitude will reincarnate in the final generation, "like in the days of leaving Egypt" (Michah 7:15). (Sha'ar HaGilgulim, Introduction 20)

According to this, the Final Redemption is really a repeat performance of the exodus from Egypt. Leaving the Diaspora will be "like in the days of leaving Egypt" because the souls then will be the same souls of the Jews who actually left Egypt with Moshe Rabbeinu. In fact, he too will return at that time as well:

> There is not a single generation in which Moshe Rabbeinu, a"h, is not there . . . in order to rectify [each] generation. (Sha'ar HaGilgulim, Introduction 20)

This is a unique situation. Most of the discussion about gilgulim deals with individuals who have reincarnated as part of their personal tikun. In some instances, husbands and wives have reincarnated together. But, an entire generation, together with the Erev Rav,[5] the Mixed Multitude, reincarnate together? This is a tikun on a far more global, historic scale.

It's as if the end of history is destined to pick up where the beginning of Jewish history left off with the death of Moshe Rabbeinu. This is when God informs him about his future return with the entire generation at the End-of-Days:

> Now you can understand the meaning of, "Behold, you shall lie with your fathers, and this people will rise up" (Devarim 31:16), which is considered to be one of the verses that has no clear explanation.[6] (Sha'ar HaGilgulim, Introduction 20)

As Rashi explains, the words "rise up" in the verse can either refer to Moshe Rabbeinu himself, that is, he will lie down with his fathers and later rise up, or to the Jewish people who will rise up, that is, rebel, after he dies. The verse is ambiguous, and it is to this that the Talmud refers.

That is only a Pshat level though. On the level

---

[5] The Erev Rav was destined to continuously reincarnate since the time of Adam HaRishon. See Session 9.
[6] Yoma 52a.

of Sod there is no ambiguity because both interpretations are intended:

> It can be explained with the words "rise up" referring to that which comes before and after them, and both explanations are true. In the future, Moshe himself will reincarnate and return in the final generation, as it says, "you will die with your fathers and rise up." The final generation, the Dor HaMidbar, will also reincarnate with the Erev Rav, and this is what the verse also says, "this people will rise up." (Sha'ar HaGilgulim, Introduction 20)

This could be because Moshe Rabbeinu is the key to the Final Redemption, and it cannot occur without him. Even though Yehoshua bin Nun led the Jewish people after Moshe's death and crossed into the Land without him, it could only be, at best, a partial redemption. This is why 850 years later the Temple was destroyed and the Jewish people were exiled to Babylonia.

Even the redemptions that followed each subsequent exile were never complete. They may have been led by great people, but they were not led by Moshe Rabbeinu himself, the only true redeemer of the Jewish people:

> The soul of Shais, in truth, was very elevated. It included the soul of Moshe Rabbeinu, a"h, and his soul is that of Moshiach. (Drushei

Olam HaTohu, Drush Aitz HaChaim, Siman 7)

Regarding the future time it says, "What has been is what will be, [and what has been done is what will be done, and there is nothing new under the sun]" (Koheles 1:9). The initials [of the Hebrew words][7] spell "Moshe," because he was the first redeemer and he will be the final redeemer. (Hakdamos u'Sha'arim, Sha'ar 6, Ch. 11)

Therefore, once it was decreed that Moshe Rabbeinu should die in the desert:

God said to Moshe and Aharon, "Since you did not have faith in Me to sanctify Me in the eyes of the Children of Israel, therefore you shall not bring this assembly to the Land which I have given them." (Bamidbar 20:12)

the Final Redemption, de facto, was delayed.

Moshe Rabbeinu's premature demise[8] was something alluded to all the way back in Egypt, before the actual exodus occurred:

God said to Moshe, "Now you will see what I will do to Pharaoh, for with a mighty hand he

---

[7] The initials of the Hebrew words of, "What has been is what will be," which are Mem-ShinHeh.

[8] Yoma 87a.

will send them out, and with a mighty hand he will drive them out of his land." (Shemos 6:1)

Now you will see, etc. . . . What is done to Pharaoh you will see, but not what will be done to the kings of the seven nations when I bring them into the Land [of Israel]. (Rashi)

This was even before the plagues began, and long before the four-fifths rejected redemption and died in the Plague of Darkness. It would seem to imply that, from the start, the exodus from Egypt was not going to be all that it was meant to be.

Perhaps this was because it was taking place 190 years earlier than it was promised to Avraham Avinu:

He said to Avram, "You shall surely know that your seed will be strangers in a land that is not theirs, and they will enslave them and oppress them for 400 years . . ." (Bereishis 15:13)

The Torah however later states at the time of the exodus:

The dwelling of the Children of Israel, who dwelled in Egypt, was 430 years. (Shemos 12:40)

. . . You must say that [the prophecy] "your

seed will be strangers" [began] when [Avraham] had offspring. When you count 400 years from the time that Yitzchak was born, you will find [that they left after only] 210 years from their [time of] entry into Egypt. (Rashi)

Why did God shorten the exile by 190 years? Apparently it wasn't for a positive reason:

Had the redemption not begun at all and they had remained enslaved to Egypt, there would not have been a rectification, God forbid, since they had entered the forty-ninth level of impurity. (Drushei Olam HaTohu, Chelek 2, Drush 5, Anaf 2 Siman 4)

Over the years living in Egypt had a terrible spiritual impact on the descendants of Ya'akov Avinu. Even though they had begun living apart from the rest of Egyptian society, it somehow infiltrated the Jewish world. The most morally decrepit society of that time drew the Jewish people down spiritually, all the way to the bottom and the 49th level of spiritual impurity.

By the time that God sent Moshe in to redeem them, the Jewish nation had been teetering on the brink of spiritual annihilation. It was his arrival together with the 10 plagues that turned the situation around completely:

Once the redemption began, from the time the plagues started 12 months prior, the Sitra Achra began to lose power. He continued to do so from that point onward, particularly from the time the actual oppression ended by Rosh Hashanah . . . In the month of Nissan, and especially on the first night of Pesach, he was completely beaten and conquered to the point of extinction. (Drushei Olam HaTohu, Chelek 2, Drush 5, Anaf 2 Siman 4)

Thus, the Egyptian exile ended early to make sure that there were still descendants of the Avos to redeem as promised. Though this is well known, few seem to wonder about the missing 190 years of exile, seemingly assuming that God just cancelled them. In truth, there is no source to say such a thing.

In fact, another name for the End-of-Days is "Keitz Hayomim," which literally means, "end of those days," as opposed to "Keitz Yomim," which actually means "end of days." This implies that the Final Redemption is not just the End-of-Days, but the end of specific days.

Which days? This is answered by the first word of the name, "keitz," which has a gematria of 190.[9] The End-of-Days, as the name implies, is the end of the 190 years left over from Avraham's prophecy about the future exile of his descen-

---

[9] Kuf-Tzaddi is equal to 100+90.

dants. Unable to survive them in Egypt, it would appear, they have been the basis of Jewish history since, and they will only end with the Final Redemption, with Keitz Hayomim.

This would help to explain why the souls of the Jews which left Egypt with Moshe Rabbeinu return at the End-of-Days. That is when they will have finally undergone their tikun and merited redemption, either through history or the final War of Gog and Magog. That is when the Final Redemption will become the completion of the first one.

This is insightful. It is also a warning. The Dor HaMidbar made some critical mistakes, such as the golden calf and the most serious of all, the rejection of Eretz Yisroel. The Jews living at the time of the Final Redemption may view themselves as unique, with new historical issues. In truth, they have the souls of an early generation, and their issues may be the same as theirs, just in modern terms.

It would be tragic to come back so late in history just to repeat the tragic errors of the past.

fifteen

moshiach & redemption

THE CONCEPT OF Moshiach, of a unique person with unique abilities who saves society from whatever it needs saving, has been a common one throughout history. Almost every culture has its own version of the same idea, even modern society with its superheroes.

The word "Moshiach" means "anointed," because the kings of Yehudah, the official lineage of royalty in the Jewish people, were anointed upon assuming the throne. The final Moshiach of the Jewish people will be from the line of Yehudah, and therefore will be anointed as king of the Jewish nation.

Being the descendant of Dovid HaMelech this Moshiach is called "Moshiach Ben Dovid," Moshiach, the son of Dovid. He will be the "final" Moshiach because one will precede him called "Moshiach Ben Yosef," an actual descendant of Yosef in the past but perhaps more of a conceptual at the time of redemption:

> I saw that my father [Rav Chaim Vital], may he be remembered for eternal life, was quite afraid of the nations of the world, that they should not kill him. After that, because of the sins of the generation it switched and he went (i.e., he died without revealing that he was Moshiach Ben Yosef) . . . (Sha'ar HaGilgulim, Introduction 36[1])

Rabbi Chaim Vital lived from 1543 to 1620. Apparently he was meant to be Moshiach Ben Yosef in his time, according to his teacher the Arizal, but it is not clear that Rav Chaim Vital actually physically descended from Yosef. From the following account, it seems as if that is not imperative to be Moshiach Ben Yosef:

> Eliyahu gave the level called the "Drop of Yosef" to Yonah Ben Amittai of Tzarephat when he revived him . . . This is also the sod of what our rabbis, z"l, have written: It was taught in the school of Eliyahu: The lad that I revived was Moshiach Ben Yosef. Since he came from a drop of Yosef he therefore will be Moshiach Ben Yosef, it should happen quickly

---

[1] This is from a footnote write by Rav Shmuel Vital.

in our time. (Sha'ar HaGilgulim, Introduction 32)

One of the famous stories of Tanach is when Eliyahu HaNavi revises the son of the widow of Tzarephat.[2] During the drought Eliyahu had been told by God to go to Tzarephat to the house of a widow who had been commanded to take care of him.

While there, the woman's son became ill to the point of death. Distraught and knowing that Eliyahu was a prophet she turned to him for help. Eliyahu took the boy aside and after praying to God was able to resurrect the child.

What is less famous is that the boy who died and was revived by Eliyahu was not just any boy, but a future prophet himself, Yonah Ben Amittai. He was the prophet sent to warn Nineveh about its eventual destruction unless they repented, and who was swallowed by a large fish along the way.

Apparently when Eliyahu revived him he gave Yonah more than just the breath of life. He also gave him a spiritual "drop" from Yosef, since he himself was Pinchas who came from Yosef,[3] and this gave Yonah the capacity to become Moshiach Ben Yosef. It spiritually connected Yonah to Yosef even if he wasn't an actual physical descendant.

The Vilna Gaon explained the role of each of

---

[2] I Melachim 17:17-24.
[3] See Session 6.

the two Moshiachs:

> In all generations, the major tasks of the two
> Moshiachs together, Moshiach Ben Yosef and
> Moshiach Ben Dovid, are self-defense, and to
> wage war against the three heads of the kli-
> pos: Eisav, Yishmael and the Erev Rav. (Kol
> HaTor, Ch. 2 Section 2:2)

Tradition teaches that God made the entire
world just to enable a free will being, man, to
choose good over evil and in doing so, earn himself
a place in the eternal World-to-Come.[4] Given the
path that human history has taken since its beginning, it is no small task.

This is because of something called the "Klipos." The word literally means "peel," because like
a peel they act as boundary, in this case a spiritual
boundary between a person and God. They are the
reality of spiritual impurity within Creation, and
they spiritually desensitize a person so that he becomes more vulnerable to sin and less capable of
relating to God and Torah.

Every negative trait or entity is the product
of a particular klipah. Thus Eisav and his descendants, representing particular traits are rooted in
one kind of klipah, Yishmael and his descendants
in another, and the Erev Rav, the Mixed Multitude, in a third. As a people, each of them exempli-
fy the trait of their specific klipah and are there-

---

[4] See Derech Hashem.

fore considered to be its chief representative.

> The specific role of Moshiach Ben Yosef is to counter Eisav, the left klipah. The specific role of Moshiach Ben Dovid is to counter Yishmael, the right klipah. (Kol HaTor, Ch. 2 Section 2:2)

As the Vilna Gaon teaches, it is the role of Moshiach Ben Yosef to overcome Eisav and the evil he brings into Creation. This is something that was identifiable the moment Yosef himself was born:

> When Rachel had given birth to Yosef, Ya'akov said to Lavan, "Grant me leave that I may go to my place and to my land." (Bereishis 30:25)

> Once the adversary of Eisav was born, as it says, "The house of Ya'akov will be fire, the house of Yosef a flame, and the house of Eisav straw; and they will ignite them and devour them. (Ovadiah 1:18). Fire without a flame is powerless from a distance, and thus once Yosef was born, Ya'akov trusted in The Holy One, Blessed is He, and desired to return [home]. (Rashi)

Whatever Eisav represents on the side of impurity, Yosef, and by extension Moshiach Ben Yosef, is the counterforce on the side of purity:

When the Jewish people are in exile, they are humbled, which is necessary for removing material baseness and bodily desires from them; this occurs through Shmiras HaBris.[5] This is the ability of Yosef,[6] and this is what Moshiach Ben Yosef will do for them. (Shem M'Shmuel, Parashas Vayishlach 5671)

Eisav is the basis of Western society, and Western society is very material. It is a culture in which physical pleasure and material status are priorities, often at a cost to Torah values. Even religious Jews exposed to the West have difficulty not being influenced by its lower level of morality and reduced modesty. Moshiach Ben Yosef will combat that influence.

The Vilna Gaon describes the role of Moshiach Ben Yosef in even more specific terms:

All the work involved in gathering in the exiles, building Jerusalem and broadening the settlement of the Land of Israel so that the Shechinah will return to it, all the principles of the work and all the major and minor details are connected to the mission and role of the first moshiach, Moshiach Ben Yosef. Moshiach Ben Yosef is the miraculous power that will assist every act done when the

---

[5] That is, by living moral and modest lives.
[6] Since Yosef withstood the temptation of his master's advances, he is considered the symbol of Shmiras HaBris.

"awakening" starts from below in a natural manner, because he comes from the earth. (Kol HaTor, Ch. 1:2)

It is the role of Moshiach Ben Yosef to kickstart the Final Redemption. As the Vilna Gaon instructed his students, an important part of this is returning to Eretz Yisroel and rebuilding the settlement, which they began to do. This will make possible and encourage kibbutz golios, the ingathering of the exiles from around the world.

It has also instigated the Arab population which is devoted to taking all of Eretz Yisroel for themselves at any cost. This battle is also being fought in Heaven:

> The ministering angel of Yishmael stood for 400 years and requested before The Holy One, Blessed is He. He said to Him, "Does one who is circumcised have a portion in Your Name?"
>
> God answered, "Yes."
>
> So he said, "Yishmael is circumcised, and [performed it] even at the age of 13. Why does he not have a portion in You like Yitzchak?"
>
> God answered him, "Yitzchak was circumcised as required and properly, but not Yishmael. Not only this, but [the Jews] 'cling' to Me properly for eight days, while the others are distant from Me for many days." He said to him [in any case], "Nevertheless, since he

was circumcised, should he not have a good reward for this?" . . .

What did The Holy One, Blessed is He, do? He distanced Yishmael from the supernal clinging, and gave them a portion below in the Holy Land, because they were circumcised. In the future Yishmael will rule on the Holy Land a long period of time, while it is desolate and empty, just like their circumcision is empty, lacking completion. They will interfere with the return of the Jewish people to their place until the merit of Yishmael has been paid. (Zohar, Vayaira 32a)

Whereas the Angel of Eisav fights against the Jewish people for its own survival and way of life, the Angel of Yishmael fights for Eretz Yisroel out of extreme jealousy. Eisav is about material desire, but Yishmael is about pride and religious status, and the Jewish people interfere with both. This shifts the battle from Moshiach Ben Yosef to Moshiach Ben Dovid:

Once the materialistic aspect and desires are removed from them, then the yetzer hara of pride and status gets stronger. It is against this that Moshiach Ben Dovid, which is Dovid HaMelech—the leader of those who humbled themselves—comes, to humble them for the service of God, may His Name be blessed. (Shem M'Shmuel, Parashas Vayishlach 5671)

This is because the outer enemy of the Jewish people is really just the projection of their inner yetzer hara. The fight against the enemy may be physical, but ultimately it must be spiritual. The nation of Yishmael comes to force the Jewish people to win both battles.

Thus when the war is primarily between Yisroel and Yishmael, it is a clear sign that the Final Redemption is in its final stage. The only question is, if the final redeemer is the reincarnated Moshe Rabbeinu:

> [Moshe] was the first redeemer and he will be the final redeemer. (Hakdamos u'Sha'arim, Sha'ar 6, Ch. 11)

how will Moshiach be "Ben Dovid" if Moshe Rabbeinu himself descended from the tribe of Levi?

Though the soul of a person has a lot to say about the destiny of a person, it does not establish his physical lineage. That is a matter of birth, and if someone born to a person from the tribe of Yehudah receives the soul of a Levi, he is a still completely from the tribe of Yehudah. He will physically be "Ben Dovid" while spiritually he will be "Ben Levi."

As to when Moshiach will come and bring the Final Redemption, it says the following:

> Once all the souls will have been separated out completely then Adam d'Klipah, which is

the [spiritual] waste [in Creation], won't need to be removed through [some kind of] action. On its own it will collapse and be "absorbed" [to the point] of not being "visible" or "present," since holiness, which is life [itself], will become separated from the spiritual waste which is called death. (Sha'ar HaGilgulim, Introduction 20)

As a result of Adam HaRishon's sin, all of the souls that were a part of him "fell off" and into the Klipos.[7] The holier the soul the deeper it fell into the Klipos. Though from man's perspective history is about the events that impact mankind for good or bad, from Heaven's perspective it is about the souls leaving the Klipos.

When the last soul has left the Klipos, the Final Redemption automatically occurs. This is because the Klipos, the source of all evil in Creation, depend upon holiness to survive, which they derive from the souls among them. When the last soul will have left the Klipos:

[They] will no longer have any life at all and will disappear like smoke, as it says, "Death will be extinct forever" (Yeshayahu 25:8). (Sha'ar HaGilgulim, Introduction 20)

In fact, the separation process is part of the responsibility of Moshe Rabbeinu himself:

---

[7] Sha'ar HaGilgulim, Introduction 7.

Thus, the initials of [the Hebrew words for] "Death will be extinct forever" are [Bais-Heh-Lamed,] the letters of "Hevel," to hint that [this will not occur] until all of the reincarnations of Hevel are completed. They are Moshe Rabbeinu reincarnating in every generation to separate out the souls from among the "waste." When this has occurred then Moshiach will come and death will be extinct forever. (Sha'ar HaGilgulim, Introduction 20)

What does this actually mean, practically speaking? How are the souls separated out from the Klipos, especially when they seem so strong at the end of history?

For the most part, this is something that remains to be seen until the entire process is over. In retrospect, it will be easier to see how the events of history occurred as they did specifically to this end. How people responded to the events of their lives is far more important than the events themselves, which are always a function of Hashgochah Pratis—Divine Providence.

The purpose of the redemption is the true redemption and the sanctification of God's Name. (Kol HaTor, Section 2, Ch. 2:2)

This is what Moshe Rabbeinu told the Jewish people before he died:

Did ever a people hear God's voice speaking

out of the midst of the fire as you have heard, and live? Or has any god performed miracles to come and take him a nation from the midst of a[nother] nation, with trials, with signs, and with wonders, and with war and with a strong hand, and with an outstretched arm, and with great awesome deeds, as all that God your God did for you in Egypt before your eyes? You have been shown, in order to know that God, He is God, there is none else besides Him. (Devarim 4:33-35)

The Talmud is more succinct when it says:
All is in the hands of Heaven except for the fear of Heaven. (Brochos 33b)

This is the choice a person has to make. When he accepts God, he falls to the side of holiness. When he rejects God, he becomes a part of the Klipos. The events of history occur as they do to compel a person to decide in which direction he wishes to go. As people move in one direction or the other, separation of holiness from impurity is achieved. When it reaches the critical point, the redemption will occur, and all that will remain will be holy.

concluding note

THE ACTUAL TEXT of Sha'ar HaGilgulim is not that long, relatively-speaking. To properly explain it though could take a thousand more pages, and still questions would remain. Its somewhat straightforward approach to a not-so-straightforward topic can be very deceiving.

The most important part of the discussion is personal tikun. As complex and distracting as daily life is it is really just the stage on which people are meant to act out their lives in pursuit of personal rectification. There is nothing else, which will become clear on each person's final day of judgment.

Too many people are unaware of this. Too many simply live from day to day without any ultimate sense of purpose or understanding of just what exactly the opportunity of life actually is. Physical survival is key, which for many includes material comfort, often at the cost of spiritual values and priorities.

Consequently people are born and later die having accomplished very little in terms of personal tikun. Many do not even think in such terms and avoid situations that are spiritually challenging thinking that nothing has been lost. This is tragically incorrect.

The point of this course was to expose people to the concept of reincarnation and personal tikun. It barely scratches the surface of the topic and can only be, at best, a stepping stone to other more detailed works about spiritual development. Every session could easily have been many times longer and a lot more detailed than it actually is.

If however this course on reincarnation inspires people to consider what their personal opportunities in life might be, it will have fulfilled its raison d'être. If it leaves its readers thirsting for a more profound understanding of life and human potential, it will have justified its existence. Most important of all, it should be acceptable to the One Who has created and maintains everything, our Creator Himself, without Whom personal rectification is a moot point.

Fundamentals of Reincarnation

15-Session Course Based Upon Sha'ar HaGilgulim

Though the original Hebrew version of Sha'ar HaGilgulim is less than 200 pages, the translated and annotated version is much longer and far more de-tailed. To make some of the material, especially sections relevant to everyday life, more readily accessible, fundamentals of reincarnation have organized into a 15-session course that is available online through Juniversity or Udemy. The course is an amazing overview of many life-altering concepts, and topics include:

- What is "Pardes"?
- What Are The Sefiros?
- The Five Levels of Soul
- What Is An Adam Shalaim?
- What is Reincarnation?
- Reasons To Reincarnate
- Leaving The Realm of Impurity

- Famous Reincarnations
- Reincarnations of Moshe Rabbeinu
- The Ten Martyrs
- Reincarnation & Resurrection
- Achieving Personal Perfection
- Return of the Generation of the Desert
- Moshiach & Redemption

The course includes PDF, Mp3, and video presentations, all of which are available through Juniversity or Udemy.

If self-knowledge, fulfillment, and personal rectification talks to you, then so will this course.

Enroll now.

Sha'ar HaGilgulim

Many cultures discuss the concept of reincarnation, but how many have an authoritative work on the topic? How many provide as much detail into the concept of personal rectification as "Sha'ar HaGilgulim," or "Gate of Reincarnations"? And how many of those works have been translated into English, annotated, and made available in hardcover, pdf, and kindle formats?

Hardcover and PDF formats available through the OnLine Bookstore at Thirtysix.org. Kindle format available through Amazon Kindle.

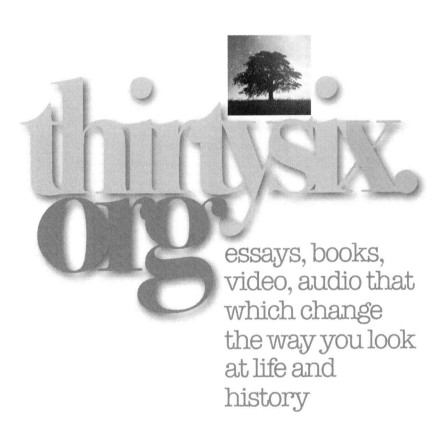

thirtysix.org

essays, books,
video, audio that
which change
the way you look
at life and
history

Made in United States
Orlando, FL
31 May 2022